Bill Barnes
August '75

Nine O'clock in the Morning

Nine O'clock in the Morning

by
Dennis J. Bennett

COVERDALE HOUSE PUBLISHERS
LONDON & EASTBOURNE

© 1970 Logos International

First British Edition 1971
Reprinted 1972
Reprinted 1973
New edition 1974

ISBN 0 902088 67 x

Printed in Great Britain for Coverdale House Publishers Ltd, 4a Balham Station Road, London, SW12 9SG by Hazell Watson & Viney Ltd, Aylesbury, Bucks

THIS BOOK IS LOVINGLY DEDICATED
IN MEMORY OF
ELBERTA BENNETT

"One of God's great ones" and
a true soldier of Christ

Acknowledgements

I want to thank all those who have helped in the offering of places of retreat in which to write: Dean and Cordie Barber, Norman and Eleanor Smaha, and Cecil and Lillian Cooper. Special appreciation for typing to Eleanor Smaha, Helen Hitchman, and Cordie Barber; thanks also to Cordie for her capable copy editing on half the book.

My thanks to the clergy, their wives, and the people of St. Luke's Church, Seattle for their love and prayers and for the faithfulness of those who have stood with me in this work through the years.

I am grateful to Christian friends all over the world who have been praying for God's blessing on this book.

Loving appreciation to my wife, Rita, who has been a full partner in this project: typing, revising, editing, and in every way lending her creative ability and encouragement. It is her book, too!

Praise and thanksgiving above all, to God Himself, Father, Son, and Holy Spirit, Who makes all things possible in His love. This is a book about Him, and how He's working through people. I pray that He will bless you in the reading of it.

In the love of Jesus,
DENNIS J. BENNETT

Introduction

How could a successful Rector of a 2,500 strong congregation risk the future of his ministry and the unity of his church by getting involved with the "baptism in the Spirit", "speaking in tongues", and all that?

And how could the same man take over a run-down mission church and see it renewed by the Spirit into one of the most spiritually alive churches in North America?

Dennis Bennett's story, told breezily in a thoroughly human and humourous style, is a powerful illustration of the movement of the Holy Spirit today.

What is this "filling of the Spirit"? What about the gifts that have recently caused such controversy? How can all this affect the lives of Christians and churches today?

This book, with straightforward narrative rather than theological explanations, will answer some urgent questions. It will show that God is just as alive and active as He was 2,000 years ago.

The marks of the Spirit's presence have always been the same: a new reality of God, a love for Jesus Christ, a hunger for the Scriptures, spontaneous joy and praise and witness, generous giving . . .

Dennis Bennett's fascinating account will undoubtedly stimulate faith in the lives of many readers.

DAVID WATSON
St. Michael-le-Belfrey, York

Contents

Nine O'clock in the Morning

I
"Fired-up" People

A day off is a good thing, and I was enjoying mine. Sunday is a busy day for a minister, and the week ahead promised to be even more so; but right now it was Monday, and I had been unwinding, pottering in my shop for most of the morning. Now, still luxuriating in the comfort of old clothes, I relaxed after lunch.

"I tell you, Dennis, there's something strange going on in my congregation!" The earnest young man with the clerical collar paused and looked at me across the kitchen table.

A fairly frequent visitor at our house, Frank was a young Anglican priest, recently come to the United States from the north of Ireland, and now, like myself, pastor of an Episcopal church in the Los Angeles area.

"Tell me about it," I said, pushing my chair back. My wife Elberta stopped clearing away the dishes and sat down to listen.

Frank riffled his hand across his close-cropped hair and shook his head ruefully.

"It's this young couple in my church," he began; "they've really got me going!"

"Whatever are you talking about?" I asked him.

Frank was silent for a moment, then shrugged.

"Well, they come to church *all* the time!" he said.

I chuckled. "What on earth is wrong with that?" I asked.

"Yes, I suppose that does sound funny; but you see, although they actually have belonged to the church for years, they hardly ever came until five months ago. As a matter of fact, I'd never met them although I became vicar of the church well over a year ago. Now they're there every Sunday, and during the week, too, if we have special events. They're just there—looking happy!"

"Looking happy in church?" I cracked. "That *is* suspicious behaviour!"

"Yes, but—well, the thing that bothers me most is that when I asked them how come they turn up all the time and look so happy, they said, 'We've been baptized in the Holy Spirit!'" *

"They've been *what* in the *what*?" I asked.

"That's about what I said when I first heard it," Frank went on. "But stranger yet, they also claim to have 'spoken in tongues,' whatever that is."

"Oh," I said, "now I'm beginning to understand what's bothering you; but why be so worried about it? There are plenty of mixed up people in the world. Expect one or two to show up in your backyard now and then. Why don't you ask them to settle down, or leave?"

"It isn't really like that," my friend replied. "You see, they

* The terms "baptized in the Holy Spirit," "baptism in the Holy Spirit," "receive the Holy Spirit" are used throughout this book. We are well aware that there is much discussion among Christians as to whether these terms should be used of the experience we are describing. We have been tempted to speak of it as "Experience X-2" to avoid argument, but that would have been clumsy! Please bear with us, and don't be thrown off the track by terminology.

don't *act* peculiar. They don't shout, or jump, or do anything wild. On the contrary, when you're with them, you just can't deny the fact that they've *got* something. They—they glow, like little light bulbs! And they're so loving and ready to help whenever I ask them. In fact, I don't have to ask them—they volunteer! They've even started tithing—you know, giving ten per cent of their income to the church!'"

"W-e-l-l, what you've described doesn't sound like too bad a disease to have spread around, Frank, barring the 'speaking in tongues' bit, of course." I rolled my paper napkin into a ball and pitched it at the wastepaper basket in the corner. My day off was getting far too complicated! Hoping to change the subject, I said brightly: "How are things going with you otherwise?"

Frank, however, was not to be sidetracked: "I know it seems odd to be worried over this business," he mused. "It certainly is strange to be upset because people are getting enthusiastic, but this 'speaking in tongues,' 'baptism in the Holy Spirit' thing bothers me. I feel I can't brush it away—I have to understand what's going on. After all," Frank paused and smiled wryly, "I *am* supposed to be the spiritual leader of the church.

"Look here!" he suddenly challenged me. "What about coming down and meeting them? See what you think?"

"Whoa! Not me, Frank! I don't want to get involved. If there's one thing I don't like, it's high pressure. These fiery parishioners of yours would probably seize me by the coat lapels and ask me if I was 'saved,' or something like that! Sorry, old friend—No! You have your little problems, and I have mine!"

Frank shrugged his shoulders again and grinned at me as he rose from the table and prepared to leave.

"Okay," he said, "I've got to get on my way. Thanks for

lunch," said he, turning to Elberta. "And, uh, see if you can get him to change his mind about coming to meet these people."

The door closed on our departing guest. I paused for a moment: "Wow! That's a wild story!" I said. "It isn't like Frank to get interested in *that* sort of thing!"

"What's the matter with it?"

I looked at my wife with some alarm: "The matter? Why it's obviously some kind of off-beat emotionalism!" I said, a little heatedly.

"But he specifically said they weren't emotional, didn't he?" Elberta queried.

"Y-e-s, but—my heavens, honey! 'Speaking in tongues!' What else could it be?"

Frank's situation left me counting my blessings. There was no "emotionalism" in *our* church! We were Episcopalians, and prided ourselves on our cool, even somewhat ironical approach to our faith. I was not eager to become involved in anything that sounded silly or irrational, and anyway, I didn't have time for it. There were, thank God, no starry-eyed zealots among my congregation—St. Mark's, in the Los Angeles suburb of Van Nuys.

Just twenty-six hundred good Episcopalians!

The Case of the "Fired-up" Parishioners refused to be ignored, though. Frank kept after me, and after a solid month of good-natured heckling on his part, I decided I might as well go and see what it was all about. My curiosity was aroused by Frank's persistence, because I did respect his judgment. Besides, I was beginning to feel a bit of a coward! At any rate, I found myself driving down the freeway with Elberta, to meet these mysterious people. It was a beautiful August evening, but I was not enjoying myself. What on earth were we getting ourselves into? I anticipated an awkward and embarrassing scene, and rather wished that it was all safely over.

I continued to feel this way as we walked up the drive to the house, a typical little California suburban bungalow. Frank was there and made the introductions. As we shook hands and sat down in the living room, I watched these people. When would they "make their move"? Then, as we talked, I began to relax somewhat, for our new acquaintances were indeed very "normal" and pleasant; in their mid-thirties: the young man quiet and straightforward; she what the women's magazines would describe as an "attractive young housewife," her dark hair and eyes contrasting pleasantly with her husband's fair colouring. The happiness and assurance that radiated from them both was unmistakable. I began to see why Frank was so intrigued.

There were the usual polite conversational openings and small talk, and then, unable to contain my curiosity any longer, I dived in:

"What's it all about?" I asked. "What *has* happened to you people?"

Without any hesitation they replied, "Why, we've been baptized in the Holy Spirit!"

"We went to a neighbourhood prayer meeting," explained Joan, her face lighting up even more at the memory, "and we enjoyed it very much." ("Good heavens," I parenthized mentally, "*enjoying* a prayer meeting? Oh, come on!") "But what impressed us most," she continued, "was this fellow named Bud. He seemed to be so happy, and so sure of God, that he made us hungry to know what he had. That's about the only way I can put it; and John felt the same." She looked at her husband, and he picked up the story:

"Yes, that's the way it was. So we asked him: 'What's happened to you?' and he just said, 'Oh, I've been baptized in the

Holy Ghost!' We didn't know what he was talking about. We didn't go to church very often—Easter and Christmas mostly —and we didn't know much about the Bible; but we were so attracted by what we felt and saw in that young man's life that we said, 'We want it, too!' "

"Yes," said Joan, "and he didn't say: 'Let's go and talk to my minister,' although he is a loyal member of a big church downtown. He just said: 'Let's pray about it. You can receive this right now.' So we did—and we *did*!"

"Get 'baptized in the Holy Ghost,' you mean," I said. "But what does *that* mean?"

"Just like in the Bible!"

That was a low blow! As a minister of the gospel—with sixteen years' experience and a graduate degree in theology from a well-known university, I was certainly supposed to know what was in the Bible. Yet as John and Joan talked, I realized that there were some very important things I'd somehow missed.

As we left their home that night, my wife, a practical person and not easily swayed, said, as soon as we were out of earshot:

"I don't know what these people have, but I want it!"

I made no outward response, but had plenty to think about. Those people had talked about God, and about Jesus Christ, with an enthusiasm that most people save for their favourite hobby, or their most deeply held political convictions! I couldn't escape the fact that these two friends of Frank's radiated something that stirred feelings and responses deep within me. They seemed to know God—to be so sure of Him. Was what I was feeling real, or was I just responding emotionally to their obvious happiness? I was rector of a large church in the San Fernando Valley and had a couple of thousand people looking to me for spiritual leadership. I didn't want to lead them down the wrong trail. Still I couldn't escape the idea that those two "fired-up" Episcopalians might have something I needed, and something others might want too, if they found out about it. But what *was* it? What did it mean?

2
Something Missing

"Well, what do you think?" My wife looked inquiringly at me across the breakfast table the morning after our encounter with John and Joan.

"I don't know," I replied, putting down my fork. "Those people sure are excited about God!"

Elberta's brown eyes became very thoughtful. She looked out of the window for a few moments before answering:

"Yes. It must be great to know Him that well."

"You know Him, don't you?" My impression was that my wife knew the Lord a lot better than I did.

"I can't remember a time when I didn't," she said slowly, "but these people seem to be so much closer. He seems especially real to them . . . I wonder how?"

I wondered too, and took my thoughts out to my study. Sitting at my desk, looking at the pile of unanswered letters, and the tentative notes that hopefully might become next Sunday's sermon, my mind swung back thirty years to my own earlier days. I *could* remember a time when I didn't know God.

My father, an English minister, brought my mother and me

to the United States when I was nine, and we settled in the little town of Campbell, near San Jose, California. As a minister's son I was brought up in "church"; yet I had not known that one could meet God personally until I was eleven years old. Elberta had been brought up in a little old-fashioned "Bible-believing" church in a northern California mill town; but the denomination in which I was raised was in the forefront of the "modernist" movement, and although I went to Sunday School and Youth Group and learned Bible stories, no one, as far as I could remember, had said anything about "accepting" Jesus Christ. Christ was presented as a great "example," and a great "teacher," but not as the divine Son of God who was also a personal Saviour.* Then one memorable night at a junior young people's meeting at our church, we had a visiting speaker, a friend of my father, an executive of the local Christian Endeavour organization. His name was Howard L. Brown.† I don't remember much about his talk, but do remember that when it ended, he looked at us eleven- and twelve-year-olds and asked:

"Is there anyone who would like to ask Jesus Christ to come into his heart?"

This, to me, was a new way of talking. Up until this time,

---

* My father, the pastor of our church, was a man who knew the Lord. He had been called to the ministry by the audible voice of God. Like many men of his generation, however, he was baffled by the outpourings of unbelief from the Biblical scholars and seminaries. It was difficult for a man of limited training to know how to react when the respected leaders of his denomination were denying the basic beliefs of the Christian faith. As a result, I was a grown man before my father shared his own experience of God with me.

† A part of Howard L. Brown's ministry was song-writing, and his name is still found in gospel song books. Having mentioned him in an article I wrote for *Christian Life Magazine* as the one who had led me to Jesus Christ, I received a wonderful letter from his widow, Margaret W. Brown, expressing her joy at finding one more person who had met the Lord through her husband's ministry.

"religion" was just a part of everyday living, like eating and sleeping. You went to church because that was what you did, that's all. Now this man was telling us that we were supposed to take some kind of step for ourselves—make up our own minds about something.

"If you'd like to ask Jesus into your heart, put your hand up," he said.

There would have been a "fat" chance of my doing any such thing, with my friends Ted C. and Bobby B. looking on, especially Bobby, who was the class humourist at school! But the man said:

"Everyone close your eyes and bow your heads."

That made it possible! Somehow I felt I *wanted* to, so I stuck my hand up. That's all I did, and that's all he asked us to do, but something happened! My heart glowed with a new warmth and happiness, as for the first time I felt the Presence of God. I had invited Jesus to come in and He had accepted the invitation!

My thoughts moved on eight years—when God suddenly broke through to me again with a "second touch." I was sitting in front of the fireplace in my father's study, reading a book I had picked up out of curiosity, which told of great men and women and their experience with God. As I read, a wonderful refreshment and joy swept through me as I recognized again the Presence of God with me.

Then in the early days of my marriage, while I was working in the electronics business, I used to get up early and sit in the morning quiet to feel God's nearness, and I would feel it! The assurance of love, warmth, and well-being that God's Presence brought, I found to be what life was all about. I realized that if I could somehow keep this continually with me, all questions would be answered. The only trouble was, I couldn't. God seemed to be gone almost before He was there. When a flash-bulb is fired, you know there has been a dazzling light because of the spots before your eyes and the latent image on the film, but the light itself is gone almost before it comes. God's Presence seemed something like that. Nevertheless, momentary though they were, these "touches" from God kept me moving in His direction.

I didn't want to be a minister, but I did want somehow to work full-time for God, so at the age of twenty-six I left my job and went back to college and then to graduate school, my purpose being to get a degree in theology, so that I would be ready for whatever field might open to me. The theological school I selected was of the most extreme "liberal humanist" persuasion, and I hadn't been there long before I found that my beliefs were to be challenged. It was, in fact, my very first night in the residence halls that my next-door neighbour, a senior, and a very "ministerial," scholarly looking chap, came by to "cue me in":

"Of course, we no longer believe in the miracles of the Bible, the divinity of Jesus, or the virgin birth," he opined, peering at me through his black-framed spectacles. "Science has shown these to be impossible, also life after death, and other such things. We can no longer accept the supernatural. We must develop a natural, scientifically respectable religion that will be accepted by modern intellectuals!" Well, his argument didn't convince me, because, having met Jesus, I knew He was the divine Son of God, but I was a bit taken aback, just the same, as I was to be many times in the following years of study!

I was to find, for example, that one of our most respected professors, a fine old gentleman and a tremendous scholar, began all of his semester classes in the psychology of religion with the preface:

"I want you to understand that I am an atheist!"

In order to support my family while I was in seminary I found it necessary to become pastor, not of one, but *two* little churches in rural Illinois, and there my family lived while I commuted home on weekends from school in Chicago, eighty miles away.

I became increasingly interested in my studies and in ministering to my churches. Strangely enough, I soon realized that theological study and church work were leading me away from my personal relationship with God. In fact, I "came to" after three years to discover that I had ceased saying any private prayers at all! I had become so concerned about study and church work that my personal life with God had become almost nil. As soon as I realized this, I did begin to say petitionary prayers again, but I was too busy for much more. It was a little like having a personal friend become your employer. You are now so busy working for him that you don't have time to spend enjoying his friendship. Your relationship has become "professional."

In 1951, two years after graduating from seminary, I had come into the Episcopal Church (Anglican), because I was dissatisfied with the vague beliefs of the church of my childhood, which seemed to say:

"A Christian is someone who agrees with the ethics of Jesus of Nazareth," or even, "A Christian is someone who says he is a Christian." I felt that the Christian faith had to be more sharply defined than that!

I soon discovered that in practice the Episcopal Church could be vague, too, but there was the great advantage that whereas the church of my earlier days no longer required its people to subscribe to "creeds and dogmas," the Episcopal Church did, so that no matter how much a layman or a priest might deny the basic truths of the Faith or the Scripture, the Creeds were there to show that he was wrong. Then too, every man ordained to the ministry of the Episcopal Church must take a solemn oath in the presence of his bishop and two other clergy, that he holds the Holy Scripture of the Old and New Testaments to be the Word of God, and to contain all things necessary to salvation.[1]

Like most converts, I went "all the way," and embraced the "high church" or Anglo-Catholic position, with strong emphasis on the sacraments, with God's grace being received objectively through the carrying out of specific actions and words—with the right intention of heart. I was happy in my work, and had plenty to keep me busy, with my growing church and growing family. Inside, however, I went on getting drier and drier. This was pointed out to me from time to time, perhaps every year or so when there would be a momentary sense of God's refreshing Presence, reminding me what it had been like to have a closer personal contact with Him. Still, it wasn't until I rounded my fortieth year, after sixteen years in the ministry, that I had really begun to face my need. I had a wonderful wife and family; I was successful in my work; yet I was dry and hungry deep inside.

In my congregation, too, I saw that while people were being helped, lives were rarely being *changed*. Because I had, for the most part, lost my personal awareness of God in my life, I wasn't able to lead the people of the congregation into that kind of awareness. I was propping them up, counselling them, encouraging them, being a "poor man's psychiatrist," teaching them about God; but something was seriously lacking. God wasn't becoming real enough to them to make any noticeable change in their lives. Their religion was a mild sedative to make their lives more palatable, rather than an experience that would drastically change them. Suppose there was something more, a great deal more, to this whole business of Christianity, and we were missing it?

The reason John and Joan intrigued me so much, I mused, was that what I seemingly had lost, they had found—only more so! I had sensed it in them as soon as we began to talk. There wasn't any getting around the fact that these two were enjoying God's Presence in their hearts *while* they were talking with us. I had never witnessed this before, and it was very exciting!

I picked up the Bible that lay on my desk and began to leaf through it. These "fired-up" people claimed to have had some kind of experience with the Holy Spirit. I had to admit that the Holy Spirit was a vague, "theoretical" Being to me. Oh, "officially," I could give a good lecture on Him; I had often done so to confirmation classes in my church, but I had never stopped to think what He was really like. Could a lack of experience with the Holy Spirit be the reason why Christians today don't show the same joy, power, and assurance that we see in the New Testament?

Maybe I'd better do a little research, I thought. So then and there I began to work my way through the New Testament— the part of the Bible that tells about the life of Jesus and the doings of the early Christians—underlining, as I went, any and all references to the Holy Spirit and His work. It was quite a job, and through the days ahead I found that there were about two hundred and forty references to the Holy Spirit in the New Testament. In his letter to the Romans, chapter 8, Paul mentions the Holy Spirit sixteen times in the first fourteen sentences! These early Christians were continually talking about the Holy Spirit; He certainly wasn't vague to them. They talked as though He told them what to do, and where to go, and what to say. They were specific about the Holy Spirit—they didn't confuse Him with the Father or with Jesus.

Another thing in the Bible that caught my attention was that the early believers had a clear-cut experience of receiving the power of the Holy Spirit. I noted that Jesus had told His first followers to stay in Jerusalem because He was going to send them power. "Pentecost" was when it first happened, but I also saw that this experience of Pentecost—of being empowered by the Holy Spirit—was repeated a number of times. Jesus told His people that they couldn't do the job He had for them until they had the power.

I saw, too, that the mysterious "speaking in tongues" kept cropping up. I counted four times in the Acts of the Apostles when there seemed to be a specific "receiving of the Holy Spirit" on the part of a group of people, and in three of the four cases it says something like:

"They began to speak in new languages . . ." [2]

In the fourth case, I found that the commentators pretty much agreed that there, too, at Samaria, they spoke in tongues.

I began to wonder how anything as definite and important as this could have been overlooked by the church today. Or had it been completely overlooked? There was confirmation.* A couple of times a year, having collected together a number of children and adults who desired to share in this rite, and given them a "cram" course in Christian faith and practice, we duly presented them to the bishop. I knew that the average Episcopalian was not too clear as to what it was all about. I wasn't! ! I knew that the major scholars of our denomination disagreed on the purpose of confirmation. I always liked the service, but didn't quite know why.

I recalled confirmation at our church several weeks previously, and pictured in my mind again the people kneeling at the altar rail, while Bishop Gooden, in his eighties but still going strong, moved quietly along laying hands on each one and praying that he would "increase in the Holy Spirit more and

* In the Episcopal, Lutheran, Orthodox, and Roman Catholic churches the term "confirmation" is used for the traditional rite intended to strengthen the Christian for service.

more." [3] In that particular class, Mrs. S., a good Presbyterian who was joining the Episcopal Church because her husband was an Episcopalian, had asked me:

"*Why* do I have to be confirmed? What does it mean?" and I had gone through the usual wheel-spinning:

"Well, er, it's the way we do it. It means you are becoming a 'full-fledged' Episcopalian! It gives us an opportunity to make sure that you know what the Episcopal Church is all about— prepares you to become a full and responsible communicant. It's a sort of solemn 'joining the church.' It's the bishop—he's the chief pastor—officially giving you his blessing." Et cetera! One could say to the youngsters:

"This is your 'coming of age,' you know." (A kind of Episcopalian "Bar Mitzvah"!)

I looked again at the "Offices of Instruction" in the Prayer Book:

"The Church provides the Laying on of Hands, or Confirmation, wherein, after renewing the promises and vows of my Baptism, and declaring my loyalty and devotion to Christ as my Master, I receive the strengthening gifts of the Holy Spirit." [4]

There it was again! Yet why was it that statistics in the Episcopal Church at large showed that fifty per cent of these same confirmands who had been prayed for to receive the "strengthening gifts of the Holy Spirit" drifted away from church altogether? What a difference from the early church where those so empowered by the Holy Spirit turned the world upside down!

One day I was browsing through the book *Doctrine in the Church of England*, which is a survey, instigated by the Archbishops of Canterbury and York, of the beliefs of Anglicans on a worldwide basis, and I came across the following thought-provoking statement:

"Participation in the Holy Spirit is set forth in the New Testament as the distinctive mark of Christians, which separated them off from the surrounding world; in the Christianity of Apostolic* times the experience described as that of 'receiving the Spirit' stands in the forefront of the Christian life, at once as the secret of its transporting joy and power and as the source of that victory of faith which could overcome the world." [5]

"Receive the Holy Spirit!" But that was exactly what Frank's enthusiastic parishioners claimed to have done! Was this then the purpose of the bishop's prayer at confirmation? Were we to expect people to be as evidently filled with the power of God as they were in the New Testament when they received the laying on of hands?

Not only did I re-examine the New Testament and the Book of Common Prayer, but I found also that the early Church Fathers, my theology textbooks, church history books, and even the hymn books now seemed to be full of references to the importance of the Holy Spirit, and a great work He was to do in our lives. How did I miss it before?

* The Episcopal Church teaches that we "continue steadfastly in the Apostles' doctrine and fellowship" which means that the same things the Apostles experienced we should expect to happen in the church today.

3
"It Came with the Package"

"Going out again tonight?" asked my long-suffering wife.

"Yep. Vestry meeting. Then I'm going to go down and visit John and Joan for a while."

"All right, I won't wait up for you."

Her smile said, "When are you going to make up your mind?"

I knew she had already made up her mind: I also knew she would not budge until *I* was ready. So once more, after vestry meeting was over, I set out for the little house in Monterey Park, where I had already spent many evenings. I just couldn't get away from the challenge of these "fired-up" people. I was both attracted and repelled. I was attracted, irresistibly, by the Presence of God that I had felt in them, and the fascinating possibility that I might come to find out for myself how one might have such a sense of His Presence. On the other hand, I was repelled by the fact that these were, after all, "mere laymen," who had a very simplistic and narrow-minded idea of the Bible. Why, they were practically *fundamentalists*, taking the Bible at face value! It was not scholarly. Then, too, they kept on about this "speaking in tongues" thing! I was quite sure I didn't want to "speak in tongues"!

This particular night I had asked a friend of mine, another priest of the diocese, to come with me. He had heard the story, and he, too, was interested.

"These people just might have something," he said, as I parked the car and we walked up to the door. "God knows the Church *needs* something!"

As we talked, and as my friend argued politely with John and Joan, I recognized a simple fact that I hadn't faced before, that in spite of my prejudices—I was on their side!

"But are you trying to tell me that you have something I don't have?" said Father C., with just a little asperity in his voice.

John shrugged slightly and smiled.

"If you didn't think we had, why would you be taking the trouble to be here?" he asked gently.

"I don't think they're really saying that," I said. "I don't think they're trying to tell us we don't have the Holy Spirit— I think they're trying to tell us that maybe the Holy Spirit doesn't 'have' us." I looked at John.

"That sounds pretty good," he said. "You fellows have to remember that we're not theologians. We can only tell you what's happened to us, and try to show it to you in the Scripture."

And this was their strong point. I had been doing my "homework," and I found that again and again as the discussion went on, I was saying:

"They're right, you know. That's what it does say in the Bible."

"But what about this 'speaking in tongues' thing?" asked my guest.

"Well," said John, "when we received the Holy Ghost, we spoke in tongues. Just like in the Bible."

There it went! Whenever we got to talking about these

things, they would drag that "red herring" across the trail!

My fellow minister didn't say anything more about it, but I hoped the "tongues thing" hadn't "turned him off." Driving home that night after dropping him at his apartment, my thoughts still ran on the subject:

Speaking in tongues! We had been told in seminary what this meant. It meant that those early Christians, who were, after all, mostly simple people, in fact, in some ways not even quite nice—got very excited and emotional, and well, you know, they made funny noises! "Ululation" was the word one professor used! Intellectuals like St. Paul were, of course, much offended by this, and told them to cool it, or do it at home if they *had* to! The phenomenon in any case hadn't lasted long, and probably was confined to those awful Corinthians!

Yet, as I had re-read my Scripture, I had seen that this wasn't quite the case. I had found that St. Paul didn't condemn "speaking in tongues," just the *mis*use of it. I found, moreover, that he freely and openly admitted that he himself did it more than the rest of them, and for some reason, considered it to be very important. I still didn't want anything to do with it! I was an Englishman by birth and nurture. I had been firmly schooled never to show my feelings. Besides, most of my courses in graduate training at the University of Chicago had been in psychology and counselling, and I knew something about hysteria, hypnosis, auto-suggestion, and stuff like that! These "tongues of ecstasy" sounded a bit too wild for me, although I had to admit that in the Greek originals of the New Testament writings about speaking in tongues, there was no mention of "ecstasy," or anything else that might indicate some kind of frenzied activity. It just said:

"They began to speak in other languages."

I hadn't yet heard anyone "speak in tongues" and hadn't the

least idea what it was all about. I just assumed it was emotionalistic and probably pathological.

Trouble was, St. Paul dragged this "red herring" around too, and even the Lord Himself had something to say about it. He said: *even Jesus*

"This is one of the things that will happen after you believe: you will speak in new tongues." [1] And St. Paul said:

"I want all of you to speak in tongues," [2] and, "I thank God, speaking in tongues, more than any of you." [3]

Of course, with my background I could easily explain away these verses. They were "later additions" to the Scripture. Jesus, although the Son of God, was also a man of His day, and shared in some of the funny ideas they had. St. Paul was catering to the pagan notions of the non-Jewish Christian converts. Neither of them had had the benefit of a modern education, nor had they read Freud or Einstein! Yet I was less and less happy with these explanations. John and Joan were uncomplicated and unsophisticated enough simply to believe the Book, and they seemed to be finding in it the key to happiness and effectiveness in a dimension I had never known. My intellect might be saying:

"You've got it wrong," but my heart was saying:

"What have you got? I want it!"

I was like a starving man circling a table on which a delicious-looking feast is spread, watching the people seated at the table obviously enjoying the food, while trying to make up his mind whether it is really safe.

Naturally I was getting hungrier and hungrier. At one point, I had almost sat down to share the feast. I had been having some conversation with Bud, the young man who had impressed John and Joan at first and had prayed for them to receive the Holy Spirit. Bud, at my invitation, had prayed with me, too, and this was the first time I heard anyone "speaking in tongues." At least, that what I understood Bud to be doing. I would never have guessed, for he was in no way "worked up," but just speaking or praying quietly in a language I had never heard. I certainly didn't do anything like that, and apparently nothing happened as he prayed with me, although I must admit that for a few days I seemed to feel a new closeness to God.

Finally, though, on a Saturday afternoon in November, after three whole months of circling, I said to my enthusiastic friends:

"Look here, I've been reading my Bible, my Prayer Book, my theology books, my church history, and as far as I can see this experience you're talking about is in them all. I want what you've got! How did you get it?"

"That's easy," said Joan, "we asked for it!"

"Okay. I'm ready to ask. Show me how!"

I don't know what I really expected from those people that day. I knew they weren't going to pounce on me—they weren't the "pouncy" kind. There were four of us present: myself, a friend of mine who was also an Episcopal priest in our diocese (not the one who had accompanied me before), and John and Joan. We were sitting in their front room, our host and hostess on the davenport under the window, I in an overstuffed chair across the room, and the other clergyman to my right. The California autumn sun was shining bright and hot outside, and the neighbourhood was fairly quiet for a Saturday, the silence broken only by an occasional car going by. I was self-conscious, and determined not to lose my dignity!

"What do I do?" I asked them again.

"Ask Jesus to baptize you in the Holy Spirit," said John. "We'll pray with you, and you just pray and praise the Lord."

I said: "Now remember, I want this nearness to God you have, that's all; I'm not interested in speaking with tongues!"

"Well," said they, "all we can tell you about *that* is that it came with the package!"

John came across the room and laid his hands first on my head, and then on my friend's. He began to pray, very quietly, and I recognized the same thing as when Bud had prayed with me a few days before: he was speaking a language that I did not understand, and speaking it very fluently. He wasn't a bit "worked up" about it, either. Then he prayed in English, asking Jesus to baptize me in the Holy Spirit.

I began to pray, as he told me, and I prayed very quietly, too. I was not about to get even a little bit excited! I was simply following instructions. I suppose I must have prayed aloud for about twenty minutes—at least it seemed to be a long time— and was just about to give up when a very strange thing happened. My tongue tripped, just as it might when you are trying to recite a tongue twister, and I began to speak in a new language!

[handwritten marginal note: how it started]

Right away I recognized several things: first, it wasn't some kind of psychological trick or compulsion. There was nothing compulsive about it. I was allowing these new words to come to my lips and was speaking them out of my own volition, without in any way being forced to do it. I wasn't "carried away" in any sense of the word, but was fully in possession of my wits and my willpower. I spoke the new language because it was interesting to speak a language I had never learned, even though I didn't know what I was saying. I had taken quite a while to learn a small amount of German and French, but here was a language "for free"! Secondly, it was a real language, not some kind of "baby-talk." It had grammar and syntax; it had inflection and expression—and it was rather beautiful! I went on allowing these new words to come to my lips for about five minutes, then said to my friends:

"Well! That must be what you mean by 'speaking in

tongues'— but what is it all about? I don't *feel* anything!"

They said joyfully:

"Praise the Lord!"

This seemed a bit irrelevant and was a little strong for my constitution. It bordered on the fanatical for such a thing to be said by Episcopalians on a fine Saturday afternoon sitting right in the front room of their own home! With much to think about, I gathered up my friend, and we took our leave. On the way to the car he said:

"I guess you must be holier than I am, because you spoke in tongues and I didn't!"

"Well, Keith," I replied, "if I've received some kind of gift, I don't know what it is. I guess I'll have to go home and unwrap it!"

Actually I felt very lighthearted—not at all embarrassed by the afternoon's events—but did not have any sense that some great spiritual breakthrough had taken place.

I thought it over for four days, not saying much even to Elberta, although I knew she was following my activities with great interest. We were alike in that we were not inclined to talk about our deepest thoughts and concerns with anyone, not even with each other, although we were very close in spirit.

It was quite late, perhaps ten o'clock the following Wednesday night, when I made up my mind to pursue the matter further, and headed my '55 Mercury down the freeway to Monterey Park, and once again knocked at the familiar door.

John and Joan greeted me warmly, but I was a little disturbed to see that Frank, their young minister who had originally introduced me to them, was there also. He was still being very "clinical" about the whole matter, and I felt embarrassed to pray for this mysterious "Baptism in the Holy Spirit" in

front of him. I felt he would be watching as if it were some
kind of lab experiment! Sensing my embarrassment, John
suggested:

"Father Bennett, why don't you and I go in the back room
and pray some more about this."

second Time

It was okay with me. I was still very much interested, and
really intrigued by my experience of Saturday afternoon. We
sat down on opposite sides of the room and began to pray.
Again there was no attempt to "work me up," no emotionalism
or excitement. Once more I prayed very quietly and cautiously,
and this time, after only about three or four minutes, words
began to come in another language, the same language, I noted,
that I had spoken on the previous Saturday—at least it sounded
like it. Again, I was in no way compelled to speak this new
tongue. It was something that I could do if I chose. I was in no
strange state of mind whatsoever, and was in full possession of
whatever wits I normally had! The dynamics of the new language were entirely under my control: whether I spoke or not,
whether I spoke loudly or softly, fast or slow, high or low. The
only thing that was not under my volition was the form of the
words and sounds that came when I chose to let them come.
After all, how *could* I formulate words in a language I didn't
know?

It was like playing the work of a famous composer on the
piano. I could play—loudly, softly, fast, or slow; and was free
to play the whole thing an octave higher or lower, if I chose;
but as long as I was playing, say Bach, or Chopin, I couldn't be
playing my own notes. I was playing *their* notes, not because I
was compelled to, but because I chose to. So it was with speaking in tongues. I was speaking the Holy Spirit's words, not
mine, but I was speaking them because I chose to, and in the
manner that I chose.

I still felt nothing out of the ordinary: no great spiritual inspiration, no special inner warmth of God's presence. It was interesting, though, and somehow refreshing, and so I spoke on for several minutes. I was about to stop, but John said:

"Don't stop. Go on. Go on speaking."

It proved to be good advice. I went on, allowing the new words to come to my lips, and after three or four more minutes began to sense something new. This language was being given me from the central place in me where God was, far beyond the realm of my emotions. Speaking on and on, I became more and more aware of God *in* me. The words didn't mean anything to me as language, but God knew exactly what they meant. God living in me was creating the language. I was speaking it—giving it voice, by my volition, and I was speaking it to God Who was above and beyond me. God the Holy Spirit was giving me the words to talk to God the Father, and it was all happening because of God the Son, Jesus Christ. As I spoke on I had a vivid mental picture of Jesus on the Cross.

I didn't have to be told to keep on speaking now, but wanted to go on, and on, and on; and I did for about half-an-hour, just letting this beautiful unknown language come to my lips, pouring my heart out to God the Father with a fluency and eloquence that I had never dreamed possible.

So many times, after praying, I had stopped with the feeling that there was so much more to be said, but I just didn't have the words. One great value of this strange phenomenon of "speaking in tongues" I discovered that night was that I could pray beyond the limitation of the intellect, telling God the things that needed to be expressed, but for which I had no words. The Apostle Paul said: "We know not what we should pray for as we ought, but the Spirit Himself makes intercession for us, with unsayable speech."[4] Again he said: "He that speaks in a 'language' isn't speaking to men at all, because no human being understands him, but mysteriously, in a way we can't really grasp, he is speaking to God." [5]

But as I spoke on, something else began to happen. My heart began to get happier and happier! The Presence of God that I had so clearly seen in earlier days to be the real reason for living suddenly enveloped me again after the many, many years of dryness. Never had I experienced God's presence in such reality as now. It might have frightened me except that I recognized that this was the same Presence of the Lord that I had sensed when I first accepted Jesus, and that I had known when I used to get up early during my years in the business world; only the intensity and reality of my present experience was far greater than anything I had believed possible. If those earlier experiences were like flashbulbs, this was as if someone had suddenly turned on the floodlights! The reality of God was something that I felt all the way through—even with my body. But instead of being fearful, I felt tremendously happy and elated.

John and I went back into the front room where Joan and Frank were waiting. I looked at them and said:

"Do you mean to tell me that a Christian can feel like I do?"

John and Joan nodded, all smiles.

"That's what we've been talking about!"

My heart was rejoicing, but I couldn't quite put my feelings into words. I just said:

"I'm floored! I'll be floored the rest of my life over this!"

What a drive home it was that night! I was still rejoicing inwardly and also overflowing with happiness. I found myself singing. I sang all the way, beginning with the traditional Introit for Pentecost: "The Spirit of the Lord hath filled the whole world, Alleluia . . . !" and ending with some gospel songs from my boyhood I thought I had forgotten.

It was well after midnight when I finally tumbled into bed.

Elated as I was, I half-expected that I would have a hard time going to sleep; instead, I fell into a deep, dreamless slumber as soon as my head touched the pillow. I don't ever remember having had such a refreshing sleep as I had that night. I awoke only once and found to my astonishment, that the wonderful happiness and sense of God's Presence was still with me. I knew that purely emotional excitement could be expected to disappear overnight. Evidently something deeper than emotion had happened to me—but what was it? Anyway, it was good, and I rolled over and went back to sleep.

4
Praise the Lord!

A boisterous mockingbird practising his latest achievements awoke me the next morning. The sun was streaming into the bedroom. My first thought was:

This good feeling of God's presence, is it still with me?

As I opened my eyes the wonderful elation of the night before filled my heart, and I said, for the first time in my life (except when instructed to do so in a formal rite of worship)—"Praise the Lord!"

I bounced out of bed and into my bathrobe and slippers. Early though it was, Elberta was already up, getting things prepared for breakfast. The rest of the family was still asleep, or at least pretending to be! I gave my wife a quick hug and a kiss.

"Guess what happened to me!"

'I wouldn't have to do much guessing, with the big smile on your face," said Elberta, dropping two pieces of bread into the toaster. "Anyway," she said, turning to face me, and smiling herself, "I knew all about it last night."

"What do you mean?" I asked, startled. "You didn't even stir when I came to bed."

"No," she said, "but a funny thing happened. I was fast asleep when you came home, but when you put your hand on the front door, a kind of jolt of power—that's the only way I can describe it—went through the house and woke me up! Somehow I knew right away what it meant, and what had happened to you. I was so sleepy that I fell asleep again waiting for you, but I knew!"

Breakfast over, I went into my study, and began to read the day's Scripture lessons. The discipline of the Church of England requires a priest to read the Prayer Book Services of Morning and Evening Prayer daily. Although the American Episcopal Church did not have such a rule, I had, for many years after my ordination, kept up the practice. Later, busyness had caused me to reduce this simply to reading the appointed Scriptures: one from the Psalms, one from the Old Testament, and one from the New. I can't say that I consciously received much inspiration from this—I was fulfilling my self-imposed obligation. After the Bible reading, I would usually pray for a few minutes. Now and then I would try to expand this prayer time, or to make a meditation, but I hadn't found much success.

On this particular morning, however, two things happened. I opened my Bible to read the Psalm and lessons, and the Word of God literally leaped out to meet me!

"Rejoice in the Lord alway, and again I say, rejoice! Let your moderation be known unto all men, the Lord is at hand! Be careful for nothing, but in everything by prayer and supplication with thanksgiving let your requests be made known unto God, and the peace of God, which passeth all understanding, shall keep your hearts and minds through Christ Jesus." [1] The words were freighted with a meaning and a power I had not felt or perceived for years. Clearly this *is* the Word of God. Then I turned to prayer, and again was amazed. As soon as I turned my attention to Him, I sensed immediately that there was a new openness between me and my Father in Heaven. He was *there* and I knew it! I prayed with assurance and confidence.

Time to go down to the office at the church: I knew that this was the place where I was likely to lose any blessing I had acquired! All kinds of petty irritating problems were bound to face me as I walked in the door.

"Oh, Lord," I prayed as I left the house, "I don't exactly understand all that is happening to me, but I know I feel wonderfully close to You. Don't let me lose it." And then I spoke in my new language. All I had to do was open my mouth, and the words were there. This time I did not get the same dramatic "lift" from it that I had the evening before. (But why should I? I was *living* at the new level.) But I spoke on, and felt refreshed.

The sexton was waiting for me at the door of my office:

"Er, Father Bennett, what do you want us to do about the chairs for tomorrow night—the parish dinner, you know?" I explained patiently how the seating was to be arranged. Thank goodness for an intelligent maintenance man!

My secretary was next:

"Mrs. A. called, and she's mad, Father Bennett!"

"Oh, what about?"

"Well, it seems she was in the hospital for two weeks and no one visited her. She's talking about cutting her pledge to the church."

I sighed. "Did she let anyone know she was ill?"

"Not as far as I can find out. Her friend Mrs. B. knew about it, but she didn't call us. You know how it goes."

"Yes, I'm afraid some people *want* to have something to complain about; or else they think the clergy are mind readers! I wonder if she waited for the doctor to hear that she was ill by hearsay, or whether she got on the phone to call him and tell him?"

My secretary grinned. "That isn't all the hot water you're in," she said cheerfully. "Little Miss C. is pretty unhappy with you, too! She said she's been away from church two weeks, and when you shook hands with her on Sunday, you didn't even say you'd missed her."

I sighed again. An average of fourteen hundred people passed that church door every Sunday, and I was supposed to know exactly who had and hadn't been there! What a public relations job!

I grinned back at my secretary: "Okay, okay. Did anything *good* happen by any chance?"

"Are you kidding? They don't call in to tell that sort of thing—just the gripes!"

The bookkeeper was standing at her office door by this time. "Hi, Father Bennett," she said brightly. "Got a minute?" I had. It was my business to have "minutes"!

"Look at this," she said, holding out a ledger sheet covered with figures.

"I'm looking," I said, peering at the hieroglyphics. "What's it about?"

"Just that we're three weeks behind in our pledged income, that's all, and that means more than $6,000. Scotty is having a fit." (Scotty was the treasurer.)

"Tell him I'll issue an order for all hands to make an impassioned appeal next Sunday," I said sardonically. Why in the world couldn't people do what they said they would for God's work, without a lot of pleading and coaxing? Well, a *lot* of it was God's work anyway!

I went into my own office and sat down, taking stock. I *still* felt good! As I paused to "catch my breath," mentally and spiritually, the joy that had been simmering in my heart came to a quiet bubble, and I rejoiced inwardly in the sweetness of God's love with me. It had never been like this before! Again, for a few minutes, I let praise overflow in the new language— letting the Spirit give me the words.

Still praising God, I began shuffling through the maze of papers on my desk; instead of feeling frustrated by the morning's complaints and the work staring me in the face, I was wishing for someone to come in the office so that I could tell about the wonderful things that were happening.

Almost immediately there came a knock at the door, and in came a little woman I knew well, a hard-working member of the church. She looked just about at the end of her tether.

"Oh, Father Bennett," she said, dropping wearily into a chair, "I just had to talk to you. I don't know what's the matter with me. I just don't seem to get anything out of my religion anymore."

"Just sit right there," I commanded. "I've got something to tell you!" And I proceeded to tell her all about what had been happening to me. Two strange things took place: one was that while I was telling her all about my experience, my own heart began to rejoice just as it had the night before; the other was that as I talked she began to look happier and happier, until finally, when I stopped, she got out of the chair and just kind of floated out of my office! Later, she began to speak in tongues. She was the first of many. I found that my counselling changed completely. Now, after a very brief getting-acquainted session, I would come to the point.

"Do you know God? Have you ever accepted Jesus?"

Often my counselling would end in praying for the person to accept Jesus, and to be filled with the Holy Spirit.

When I left the office shortly before noon I was utterly amazed to find that my joy was still with me, and that I drove my car down the highway with the waves of God's love just pouring over me!

The following night was one of those rare luxuries, an evening at home with the family. I was enjoying playing a game of "Monopoly" with Elberta and the kids, and had just acquired both Boardwalk and Park Place and was ready to build some hotels, when the phone rang:

"Father Bennett, can you come out right away? Grandpa died very suddenly this afternoon!" It was the father in one of the faithful families in the parish. The grandfather had died unexpectedly and without warning. It was a very closely knit family, and all were greatly upset.

I hurriedly set out for their home. I always dreaded this kind of call. What can you say to a family at such a time? I would usually just go and sit and offer my sympathy in silence, rather than be betrayed into banalities. Tonight it was different. As I drove along, I praised the Lord and prayed, in English and "in the Spirit." Arriving at the house, I was confident because of the vivid sense of God's presence with me; and as I sat in the room with that family and began to talk as the Lord gave me the words, I was strongly conscious that I was saying the right things to bring comfort and understanding. Even the young grandchildren were listening with close attention, and when I left the house that night, the father of the family wrung my hand, saying:

"We cannot say thank you enough. You said just the right things."

This new awareness, which amazed and delighted me, seemed to pervade my sleeping as well as my waking life. The great spiritual directors bemoan the fact that though a person may try to please God while awake, when he falls asleep, it often seems the devil has free reign! How can a man be a Christian in his dreams? Up to this time, my dreams had been

Dream life changed

like most: mixed up, sometimes frightening, never making much sense, except as they might express frustration, fear, or suppressed desire. Now, suddenly and immediately, my dream life changed as sharply as my waking life. I began to think about God in my dreams, and to function as a Christian asleep as well as awake. The same standards of morality began to apply in my dreams as in my waking life! I found that if I had a bad experience in a dream, I would call on Jesus for help. Often I would dream I was praying for the sick, preaching, casting out evil spirits, and most wonderful of all, I would dream I was praising God! Other nights I would awaken just knowing that God had been refreshing me while I slept, without my being able to remember exactly how, but knowing He had been there just the same.

All these things were wonderful beyond description, but very soon something else happened, just as important. Like most Christians, I suppose, I had often tried to surrender my life to God. Somehow it had never seemed to "work." I could say all I wanted about "yielding" and "commitment," but the fact was that my life always seemed to come bouncing back into my own hands very quickly. I was thinking about this early one evening as I drove down Sherman Way past St. Mark's Church. The road, wet with an autumn shower, was gleaming in the last glow of the fading sky, and the reflection of the newly-turned-on street lights. As I approached the big intersection at Van Nuys Boulevard and prepared to turn left, suddenly I said:

"Lord, I do surrender my life to You. I do consecrate myself to You!" Many times before I had said it, but this time something happened! It was as if God had replied immediately: *alone in car*

"All right! I'll accept your offer!"

My reaction was not typical for me, for so vivid was the experience that I started to weep, and had to pull the car over to the side of the road while I regained my composure. In that

surrender

moment I knew, to my great joy that God *had* accepted my offer and that there was no way to back out of it even if I had wanted to, and I surely didn't! God had freely given me the gifts of Salvation and Pentecost, and now I offered to Him the only thing I had to give—myself.

5
A Glorious Fellowship

Late one evening, about three days after my "Pentecost," Frank called me:

"Dennis, we've found another Episcopal priest who speaks in tongues!" he announced. "He's going to meet with us to-night! Can you come?"

Frank called not only me, he also called all of the people who had recently received the Holy Spirit at his church. It was a group of fourteen Episcopalians who came to a home in Monterey Park to meet a youngish man from Texas whose round collar proclaimed him to be a minister. He told us a little about himself and how he had received the power of the Holy Spirit a number of years before. Of those others present, all but two had been baptized in the Holy Spirit, and ironically enough, one of the two was Frank, the one who had called this whole matter to my attention in the first place. Frank had been saying to the rest of us:

"You go and try it, and see what happens to you!" but had himself been keeping his "objectivity," although getting warmer and warmer! He said to the Texas priest:

"Now don't you pray for me tonight! I'm going to pray *tomorrow* to be baptized in the Holy Spirit, but not tonight!"

As the young Texan talked, Frank became increasingly tense. I could feel it, as if I were seated next to a tightly coiled spring! Occasionally he would whisper some comment in my ear: "This is silly!" he said. Then our visitor began to pray. I had never heard anyone pray quite as he did. He was very informal, almost "chatty" with God. He didn't use Prayer Book language, or "thees" and "thous," and he didn't go through elaborate descriptions: "Almighty God," "Most Gracious Lord," etc. He just said: "Dear Father . . ." as if he really felt that way! As he prayed something began to happen: my spirit began to leap for joy within me. The nearness of the Lord which I had been feeling so much was intensified. It was as though the Glory of God came down and tangibly rested upon that little circle of people. Then I realized that the others were feeling the same way. People—good old-line stuffy Episcopalians, too! —were beginning to chuckle to themselves with joy, or weep quietly, as they felt the amazing reality of God's love. God was so definitely *there* that we felt we could almost reach out and touch Him.

In spite of my own joyous involvement, I could not help but notice the reactions of the two men who had not yet received the Holy Spirit. Frank was getting more and more tense, while the layman who had not yet received (he did shortly afterward), was looking around with a puzzled stare trying to comprehend why his friends were behaving so strangely. It was evident that neither of them was feeling the tremendous joy and love that the rest of us were sensing.

Suddenly the leader began to pray for Frank. He didn't mention him by name, but he prayed for him to be baptized with the Holy Spirit. The effect was almost immediate. After perhaps thirty seconds, Frank leaped to his feet, as in a glorious torrent a new language poured from his lips. I have never heard anyone speak more rapidly! He stood up. He sat down. He began to walk around the room, forward, then backward, and all the time the praises of God were pouring from him in a rush of new and unknown words. He was caught up in the glory of God. The rest of us just plain rejoiced! It was wonderful, it was glorious, and it was funny, too, with a kind of divine humour. We even clapped one another on the back as we said:

"Praise God! Isn't He wonderful!" It was like all the birthday parties in the world rolled up into one!

To look at Frank, one would have thought that he was completely "out of it", in "ecstasy", but as a matter of fact he was nothing of the sort. He was enthralled with God, but he was in full possession of his senses. This fact was demonstrated when suddenly, right in the middle of his outpouring, he stopped and said, in a matter-of-fact way:

"Well, I always said that if ever I spoke in tongues, I had a little poem ready for the occasion!" Frank loved to write humorous verse, and out he came with a parody of the song from "My Fair Lady":

> "I spoke with tongues all night,
> I spoke with tongues all night,
> And praised the Lord all day ..."

Then he immediately went back to pouring out his love to God in an unknown language, and we could scarcely get another word of English out of him that evening!

If we haven't found just being with God the most enjoyable and all-satisfying experience on earth, whatever will we do in

Heaven? Will we have to play interplanetary golf, get a trans-lunary game of bridge going, or interest ourselves in a heavenly workshop, in order to relieve the boredom of "just" enjoying fellowship with God?

For me up until now, as for most Christians, a prayer meeting had sounded about as exciting as a funeral! I had never belonged to a church that had one! (My parish had a prayer group which met to read long lists of names, and say some set prayers for the sick. It was a sincere effort and not without results, but far from exciting!) Now this new and wonderful fellowship with God and with one another began to take priority in our lives. We met together to pray, not out of a sense of duty, but because it was more wonderful than anything else we had ever experienced. God was with us, and everybody knew it, and shared it.

The first prayer meetings centred around praying for people to receive the Holy Spirit, for we soon discovered that just as Jesus had said, all who asked, received. At first there had been a steady trek down to John and Joan's house, but we soon learned that the Holy Spirit could be received just as nicely at Bob's house, or Don's house, or even at the rectory! Meeting to pray with a new "candidate" would so inspire everyone all over again, that we would go on praising God, and loving Him together, long after the newly baptized-in-the-Holy-Spirit Christian had begun to praise God in a new language. Then we began to get together for the express purpose of fellowship, whether there was anyone to be prayed with for the blessing of Pentecost or not, just because it was so wonderful to experience God's love.

These home meetings would begin very casually. There was no attempt at formal procedure. The first half-hour would be spent just chatting and drinking coffee. The air would be blue with smoke from half-a-dozen cigarettes and a pipe or two—

for Episcopalians at that time saw no connection between smoking and religion, pro or con!*

Singing came very naturally into the picture. I remember the first night I came bringing a gospel songbook. Many of these folks had never heard a gospel hymn. They were raised on "good music"! I have nothing against the beautiful cadences of a Bach chorale, or the good poetry in a beautiful hymn, but these things are "set pieces", fine for the professionals to sing. If you want a group of just plain everyday folks to enjoy singing, give them something they can clap their hands to, something with dotted eighths, and lively rhythm.

"Why should the devil have all the good tunes?" asked General Booth—and we say, "Why indeed?" At any rate, these "high church" Episcopalians discovered gospel music, and they loved it! Then they discovered choruses—little short songs that could be learned quickly and could be picked up and sung at any point in a praise meeting.

As the meeting progressed, someone would strike up a chorus, or a gospel song. Coffee cups and cigarettes would be laid down, and we were on our way. The singing might con-

---

* I myself had been a light smoker until I received the Baptism with the Holy Spirit. At that point I found it a physical impossibility to smoke! We did not find it necessary to make an issue about it. One by one, people who had received the Holy Spirit would stop smoking—without being told to, until it became rare to see anyone smoke in our fellowship. This has puzzled me a bit. Clearly, many who stopped smoking had far worse habits and problems that needed dealing with: overeating, and other overindulgences of various kinds, to say nothing of gossip, lack of honesty, conceit, and all other sins fallen mankind is heir to! The best explanation I can offer is that such things as overindulgence in smoking, or drinking, bad language, etc., are the outward symptoms of deeper problems. Being outward, they can be dealt with outwardly. It takes much longer to change the inclinations of the heart. It is important that these outward patterns be changed, but it is important not to make the mistake of thinking, as many do, that a change in these outward habits means "holiness." Holiness is a matter of the heart.

tinue for a half-hour or even an hour, and this was a clear sign that something pretty basic had happened. These folks who wouldn't have opened their mouths to sing the national anthem at a ball game, or a graduation ceremony, and whose attempts at hymn-singing on Sunday morning had been the despair, no doubt, of generations of clergy, now didn't want to stop. Chorus would follow chorus, and it was a rare evening in which a new song or two was not learned.

After the singing came another completely new thing, praise. Not thanksgiving, but just plain praise, which not only permeated the meetings but our personal everyday affairs also. The prophet Isaiah wrote:

"In the year the King Uzziah died, I saw also the Lord, sitting upon a throne, high and lifted up, and His train filled the temple. Above it stood the Seraphim: each one had six wings: with two he covered his face, and with two he covered his feet, and with two he did fly. And *one cried unto another* and said:

" 'Holy, Holy, Holy, is the Lord of Hosts! The whole earth is full of His glory!' " [1]

A few weeks after I received the Holy Spirit, a phone call came from my church librarian. She was a well-educated person in the best sense of the word, a gracious and cultured lady, and she had just received the Holy Spirit a day or two before.

She said: "Good morning, Father Bennett. I would like to talk with you about some books."

I replied: "Good morning, Madelyn. Praise the Lord!"

She said: "Amen! Glory to God!"

I said: "Praise God!"

She said: "Blessed be His Name!"

I said: "Amen!"

We went on like that for perhaps five minutes, caught up in

praising and glorifying God back and forth over the telephone! We too were, in a small way, sharing the experience of the seraphim around the throne. At length I said: "Madelyn, we've got to talk about books!" It was only with a real effort that we could wrench ourselves away from that joyous fellowship to give our attention to such mundane things.

This new activity of praising God was seen to be the source of power and freedom in our meetings.

"Father, I love you!" "Jesus, You're wonderul!" "Blessed be God!" "Glory be to God!" "Thank you, Jesus!" "Hallelujah!" Perhaps twenty or thirty persons at a time could be heard spontaneously uttering words of praise. Most eyes would be closed, some faces lifted to heaven, a number of hands raised in this ancient gesture of prayer. The voices blended in a murmur that surely the writer of the book of Revelation might have had in mind when he spoke of the "sound of many waters." Such praise might continue for five minutes, or ten, and be repeated several times during the evening.

In such a setting it was only natural that we would pray, but it was a different kind of prayer. The old formalities might be all right in church—and these people were faithful, every-Sunday churchgoers—but formal prayer didn't somehow fit with the intimate fellowship we felt with God and one another. It just wasn't like that. Paul said that the Spirit of God in us would make us cry out "Abba!"[2] "Ab" is an Aramaic word meaning "Father" in the formal sense, and "Abba" is the child's word for the same thing, more like "Daddy." So our prayers were childlike and simple, conversational—talking with the Father in a new freedom—but strangely enough, far more powerful and effective than anything we had seen before.

It was at such a gathering, about a week after my initial experience with the Baptism in the Holy Spirit, that we prayed with Elberta. She had been quite ready to receive the Holy

Spirit ever since the first evening we spent with John and Joan, and now that I had been baptized in the Spirit, there was nothing holding her back. As we gathered around her and prayed, the Holy Spirit filled her so full that when she tried to get up from the chair she was sitting in, she staggered from the sheer weight of joy and glory of God, but she couldn't break through the "sound barrier" to speaking in a new language!

"Ab, ba, ab, ba . . ." was the best she could manage, but it was a good beginning, for unknown to her intellect, her spirit was crying as a child, "Dear Father!" It was a wonderful and natural way to start, but she couldn't seem to get any further.

"I got a 'D' in Spanish in high school, because I wouldn't open my mouth and say the words," she said. "I guess this is sort of the same thing!" Elberta was filled right up to the brim, but longed for the full freedom of the Spirit, and the overflow of her heavenly language.

In the meantime, many friends in the parish were continuing to receive the Holy Spirit.

"There's the phone!" It was nearly midnight. "I wonder who that could be?"

"Dennis!" the voice at the other end of the line said. "Mary received the Holy Spirit two hours ago and has been speaking in tongues ever since! Boy, is she getting a blessing! We just had to call and tell you!"

"Well?" Elberta looked ot me a little grimly, as I hung up the telephone. "Someone else?"

I nodded.

Elberta sighed. She knew that these people were coming into a freedom and joy in the Lord that she didn't yet have, and she knew it had to do with that tongue of hers that somehow wouldn't loosen up!

It was six weeks later that I came home late one night from a meeting and found Elberta waiting for me.

"You still up, honey?" I asked. "It's after eleven."

I took another look at her. The joy on her face told me the story. I raised my eyebrows questioningly:

"Did you?"

"Yes!" she said happily. "I got my new language tonight!"

"How did it happen?"

"Oh, I just knelt down at the bed to say my prayers, and I said, 'Lord, I'm not going to get up until I speak in tongues.'" She chuckled. "I shouted for a while, and it sounded pretty silly. Then I whispered a while, and that didn't seem to do any good either. Then I fell asleep on my knees, and when I woke up, I was talking to Him in a new language!"

At our weekday meetings there would be a good deal of "speaking in tongues", but most of it would be inaudible, or nearly so, except during times of general praise, when people might speak out in the "unknown tongue" praising God, just as others would be speaking in English. Now and then during such an evening some one or another, not more than the scriptural "two or three," might be moved to speak out in their Holy Spirit language, in which case everyone else would stop and listen, and then wait for the interpretation, which St. Paul says must follow a public message in an unknown tongue. This means that someone, either the speaker in tongues or some other person, would be given by the Holy Spirit the general meaning—not a word-for-word translation necessarily—of what had been said in the unknown language. I have heard an interpretation brought in sections by as many as five people, seated in different parts of the room. One of those interpreting stopped right in the middle of a phrase, and across the room another picked up the sentence without a moment's pause. I knew the speakers did not know each other, and could not possibly have rehearsed what they did; yet it would have seemed impossible to have joined the sentence so smoothly without collaboration!

At another meeting, there was an interpretation following a "speaking in tongues", and after it had been given, another person said:

"Father Bennett, I just wanted you to know that I had that same interpretation too." I then asked:

"How many in the group had similar words given them?" Seven hands went up! It is hard, in the face of such evidence, not to see that this was the Holy Spirit at work.

Besides tongues and interpretation, there would be prophecy, which in the Bible is not "fore-telling" but rather "forth-telling": God speaking to His people supernaturally but in a known language, to encourage and strengthen and bless them, and sometimes sharing His plans for the future with them. The gift of prophecy is not looking into a "crystal ball," or "telling fortunes," but God revealing what He is going to do! Someone would feel led to bring words of encouragement, such as:

"The Lord would say to you, 'My child, your life is like fabric. On the outside it looks smooth, and well made, while on the inside you know too well the knots, snarls, and roughnesses that are there. If you will let Me, I will make your life like Mine, of fine twined linen, like damask—beautiful on the inside as well. Let Me weave My character into the fabric of your life. I will fashion that which pleases Me, and you shall know My hand on your life in a new way. My child, I love you! You shall truly be My workmanship and be made in My likeness.' "

"Praise the Lord!" There would be a ripple of praise throughout the group. Certain people would find such words as these especially meaningful to them. Perhaps they brought home something special God had been speaking to them about that week, or that very day. A joyful chorus or two would usually follow these words of edification. Such meetings might well go on until 1.30 a.m., and then break up only because people *had* to go home. A group of hardy souls might continue further, sometimes until 4.00 o'clock in the morning. Quite a bit different from the old way of life—and other kinds of parties continuing until the wee hours, and maybe a hangover to follow!

All this was very exciting, but perhaps the most impressive thing about it was that the lives of these people began to change. A new love and concern began to be shown among them, and from them to others. They showed the same willingness to help and to be involved that those first people to be baptized in the Holy Spirit had shown in Frank's church. Suddenly, in a very practical way, they were "part of the answer" instead of "part of the problem."

6

More to the Package

One evening a few days after I had received the Holy Spirit, Elberta met me at the door looking concerned and a little exasperated:

"Conrad's got a problem," she said. "You know he was supposed to go to a party tonight. . . ."

"Uh-huh. What's the matter?" Conrad, our youngest child, age twelve, was scheduled for his first "dress up" affair, a supper-birthday party at the home of one of his friends. His first real dark-suit, white-shirt, necktie ensemble was the sensation of the week at our house!

"Well, you know Con. He got into his new suit early, and then had to go out and fool around in the yard, playing with the cat. Duffy got up in the tree. Conrad tried to get her down and in the process got a small piece of bark in his eye. I got the thing out of his eye, all right, but it seems to have scratched his eyeball. I don't think he'll be in any shape for the party; it's hurting him too much."

I murmured something sympathetic and then went down the hall to wash my hands for supper; on the way back I looked in on the unfortunate. He was lying on his bed, very glum, with a pad of witch-hazel-soaked cotton on his eye.

"Too bad, kid," I said. Without thinking too much about it, I put my hand on his head and prayed under my breath, then came into the dining room, and sat down at the supper table.

"Funny thing," commented Elberta a few minutes later, coming to the table herself after a brief stop at Conrad's room, "he's perfectly okay. His eye suddenly stopped hurting him and he's going to the party after all!" To confirm her words Conrad emerged, grinning happily, with a beribboned present under his arm.

I didn't say anything to Elberta about the prayer, but my own eyes came open a little wider. Healing? Was this "part of the package" too?

At our church I suppose we must have prayed for at least a thousand people a year to be healed of one ailment or another. We had a special "healing service" each week on Thursday morning, following the Communion, and from time to time had invited someone or another to conduct a "healing mission". It was only a few months since we had had such a mission with a well-known leader from England. It had been an inspiring week, and the man had given some excellent talks on the healing power of God. Hundreds of people had come to hear him, and many of them had come to the altar rail for prayer. I am sure that many of these were much helped, and undoubtedly there were healings we did not hear about, but on the last night of the mission Elberta put into words the question that had been bothering me:

"It's been wonderful," she said, "and I know a lot of people have been helped and encouraged, but—" She looked at me for a moment. "Where are the healings?"

Then I realized that she, like myself, had been hoping against hope that someone would get up from a wheelchair, or throw away his crutches, or give some definite sign of healing such as we read about in the Bible.

I used to kneel at the altar rail of the church and say:

"Lord, where is the power You promised us?"

My role as a sort of "traffic policeman," determining which people needed more expert help than I was equipped to give, and using my psychological training to play the "poor man's psychiatrist" for those who didn't seem too upset or disturbed, had sometimes bothered me:

"You are too sick for me to help you, Mrs. Smith, so you must go to the doctor."

"You are too disturbed for me to help you, Mrs. Jones, so you must go to the psychiatrist."

"Your family is in too much of a mess for me to help you, Mr. and Mrs. Brown, so you must go to the family counselling board, or to your attorney." That was the way it seemed to go.

I had often asked myself: "If you are a personal representative of Jesus Christ, why are you just a 'referral bureau' for hard cases?"

When Jesus met a sick man, He did not say to him:

"Here is my card. I know an excellent doctor in Jerusalem who specializes in your kind of problem. Tell him I sent you!" When He met the wild man of Gadara, He didn't say:

"My friend, you need to see a good psychiatrist. I recommend Dr. White down in Jericho. He will not charge you too much for group therapy sessions!" No. He dealt with these problems by the immediate power of God, and He told His followers they were supposed to do the same.

"Go on out," He said. "Heal the sick . . . raise the dead, throw out evil spirits . . ." [1]

Yet there had been times when we saw that power. Now and then, every year or two, an unmistakable healing would take place. I well recall the time one of our vestrymen was told by his doctor, a good friend of mine, that he had a carcinoma of the throat. The doctor asked me for help in preparing the man psychologically and spiritually for surgery to remove his pharynx. We tried to counsel him, but we also anointed him with oil and laid hands on him for healing. I shall not forget the excitement and baffled delight of the doctor when he called me to say:

"I don't know how to account for it. I *know* this man had a cancer of the throat, but now he doesn't!" (I find, by the way, that many times doctors are quicker to acknowledge God's healing power than ministers are!) That was a great day, but such days were all too infrequent.

Was the little incident of Conrad's eye an indication of what would follow? I wondered to myself. Could it be that this "Baptism in the Holy Spirit" had something to do with the release of that kind of power? It seemed so.

One day, shortly after this, Dorothy, a faithful church member, hobbled to the altar rail and asked for prayer. She had broken her hip in an automobile accident; it had healed imperfectly, and the doctor told her she would never walk normally again, or without pain. When we laid hands on her *healed* and prayed, the hip was instantly healed. That afternoon, her husband, a devout sceptic, called me:

"Dennis, I don't know what's going on over there, but Dorothy's hip is completely normal. She can move her leg in any direction, and without pain!"

About the same time another of our members presented herself for prayer. She had an ugly eczema or psoriasis covering her hands. We prayed; and I wish I had not looked away for a moment, for when I looked back, the unsightly lesions were all gone. The skin was as clear as a baby's.

Sometimes it seemed that nearly everyone who asked was healed, and why not? Jesus had said:

"These signs *shall* follow them that believe, they *shall* lay hands on the sick, and they *shall* recover." [2] No "ifs," "ands," or "buts" about it! And the power to heal the sick was not confined to a special group of people such as the ordained ministry, but was to be exercised by "those who believe."

It was very understandable, with such things happening, that in addition to prayer and praise, a good deal of our time at our meetings should be taken to tell what God had been doing in people's lives: "testimony," to use the old-fashioned word. Such sharing might go on for an hour or more:

"I prayed for my daughter's sore throat, and it was healed!"

"I burned my hand on the stove, and my husband prayed for it. I don't even have a blister—look!" And the hand was held up for inspection to the glory of God!

It wasn't just God's healing that people were discovering, but also His guidance and help in other areas:

"I was out of a job, but God found me a better one! Praise His Name!"

"We had been having real problems in our marriage, but God has just cleared it all away, and it's like we were on our second honeymoon!"

Less dramatic, and yet in a subtle way more so, was the testimony of the person who just stood up, and with the joy of heaven on his face would say:

"I just want to thank God for being so close and so real to me!"

Jesus said we would be witnesses after we received the Holy Spirit, and sure enough that's what began to happen. God was becoming so real and so wonderful that we wanted to tell others about the joy that had come to us, and the Holy Spirit had set our tongues free to do the telling! So we would have testimonies like this:

"The girl that works at the desk next to mine at the office had a terrible headache. I asked if I could pray with her, and she looked at me funny, but said: 'Yes, it couldn't do any harm,' so I prayed for her and the headache went away. She said: 'How come?' and I told her about Jesus. Now she's accepted Him and she's happy as a clam! She and her husband were fighting all the time and were on the verge of divorce, but she told him about Jesus, and he's interested. They're coming to our house tomorrow night to talk about it some more. Pray for us, will you?"

Sometimes nearly everyone in the room had some kind of a report to give: not what God did years ago, or even last year, but what He did last week, yesterday, today! Since the Bible had come alive to them in a new way, some would share a Psalm or other Scripture that had been significant to them. Then, with faith built higher by this sharing, the group would plunge back into prayer, singing, and praise.

7
Clouds Roll In

"Hey, Bob! How are you?" a vestryman greeted a friend at the coffee hour following the service at St. Mark's Church one Sunday morning late in 1959.

The answer rang out only too clearly across the ranks of loyal churchmen sipping their coffee:

"I'm fine. Praise the Lord!"

And then, as if to add insult to injury, came the response from the other.

"Praise God!"

Most of the company ignored the speakers: here and there glances of amusement or mild surprise were exchanged—this wasn't the usual kind of greeting heard on a Sunday morning! But the closer observer might have seen some brows furrowed with real irritation.

"What's going on in this church? Fanaticism!"

It was the first distant rumble of a storm that was to gather with astonishing rapidity and break about my head. To have "trouble" at St. Mark's would have been incredible to me. When I accepted the "call" in 1953, St. Mark's had been a church of some five hundred members, just recovering from serious difficulties. During my seven years as pastor, the Van Nuys area had undergone tremendous growth, as the sprawling City of Los Angeles overflowed into the San Fernando Valley. The church had grown with the population.

I had three assistant ministers on my staff, capable and trusted men, one of whom had been with me throughout my pastorate; in fact, he predated me, having been interim pastor before I came. One day, as was our weekly custom, the four of us were meeting at lunch to discuss the parish and its work. Toward the end of the meal, my senior assistant suddenly said:

"I understand people in our church are now speaking in tongues!"

My "number two" man grinned. "That's what I hear," he said. "What next?"

My heart flipped. "Wait a minute," I said. "I just want you fellows to know that I take this very seriously."

The older priest dropped the subject, but "Number Two" looked at me sharply. After lunch he walked with me back to my car.

"Do you speak in tongues, Dennis?" he asked seriously.

I nodded.

"I'd like to talk to you about it sometime," he said.

Inwardly, I heaved a sigh of relief. I had hesitated broaching the subject to these two fellow workers of mine. They were men of experience in the ministry, men whose earnestness and sincerity I respected. Now that the subject had been brought up, I felt I could relax; for my third assistant, a young fellow just out of seminary, and his wife had recently been baptized with the Holy Spirit and were eagerly sharing in the fellowship.

Things seemed to be moving along very nicely, which suited me just fine, for I was by preference a compromiser, not a fighter. However, I was underestimating the enemy. Most Christians are half-inclined to think of Satan as a legendary figure, but the Bible says that immediately after the Lord Jesus Christ received the power of the Holy Spirit, just following His baptism in Jordan by John the Baptist, the Spirit drove Him into the wilderness where He was tempted by Satan. All you need to do to be convinced of Satan's reality is start getting Christians empowered with the Holy Spirit. I soon was to discover this for myself.

As word began to spread that some people at St. Mark's were "speaking in tongues," fear and prejudice was stirred in the hearts of a small group of well-meaning but poorly informed folk, who determined to set themselves flatly against this experience. It wasn't long before all the standard rumours were flying: St. Markans were holding secret conclaves in the dead of night, at which there were all kinds of strange goings-on. It sounded like pretty exciting stuff, and there is in fallen human nature a perverse love of scandal which feeds on such talk. Actually nothing untoward or out-of-hand was happening; it was just that Christians were discovering how wonderful the fellowship of the Holy Spirit could be. The people who were the targets of the gossip were among the most faithful members of the congregation. After about sixty people had received the Spirit, we had taken a little census and found that these few persons were supporting ten per cent of the budget of the entire church. They included the junior warden of the parish; another member of the twelve-man vestry or official board; several of our most active and faithful laymen who for years had been turning out at six o'clock every Saturday morning to share communion and study their faith in order to be better witnesses for Christ; the directress of the Altar Guild, and her assistant; the president of our most active Women's Guild; and the church librarian. But position and reliability made little difference. As soon as a person, no matter how respected, was known to be involved, he or she was on the "list." "Look out! They've got it, too!"

Once I asked one of my associates who was very antagonistic to the Baptism with the Holy Spirit:

"What do you think of Mrs. C.?" I had named a very charming and intelligent younger woman of the parish.

"Why, I think she's a fine person, of course."

"Well, then. why don't you have a talk with her?" I asked. "She speaks in tongues."

He looked at me indignantly. "Then I don't *want* to talk to her!" he declared.

It was ironical that while clergymen were reacting in this manner, men of other professions, perhaps even better equipped to judge human mental and physical health, were reacting quite differently. It was too bad that my assistant could not or would not talk with the husband of my Altar Guild directress.

He was a well-known neuro-surgeon in the San Fernando Valley, and after his wife received the Holy Spirit, I anticipated a strong reaction from him. One day I called him to discuss a person in the parish who seemed to be having a neurological problem. When we were through talking about the patient, the doctor said:

"Oh, by the way, I see what's happening to my wife, and I like it!"

I did a "double-take": "You *do*?"

"Yes," he replied. "You're going to have a hard time explaining this 'speaking in tongues' to some people, though." He paused a moment and then added casually:

"Of course, I understand it."

I was so surprised that I simply said again: "You do?"

"Sure! You see, the speech centres dominate the brain. If they were yielded to God, then every other area would be

affected, too. Besides," he continued, "I think about God sometimes, and I run out of words. I don't see why He shouldn't give
me some additional words to use."

Much is being said today about the "generation gap." Ten
years ago the cliché hadn't been invented, but parents were
already pretty well sold on the idea that their children were
potential delinquents who might become unmanageable at any
time. The cult of the "terrible teenager" was thriving, and
Satan used it to further his purposes.

One Sunday night my youngest assistant called me:

"I'm sorry, Father Bennett. I didn't mean to cause any
trouble."

"What are you talking about, Jim?" My heart sank. I was
growing tired of crises.

"Well, I stopped by the drugstore after the young people's
meeting and Susan and Walter were there. They asked me,
'Father Jim, what is all this about the Holy Spirit?' All I did
was to tell them what God had done in my life, that's all. But
something has happened to *them* both. They're just sitting there
as if they're overwhelmed by the whole thing. What'll I do?"

So here it comes! I thought. People had already been
whispering, "Supposing the kids should get hold of this 'speaking in tongues' stuff? It's just like a drug, you know. That's why
these folks get together so often. They have to have this whatever it is."

Even I and others who had received the Holy Spirit had
felt a little apprehensive about our kids finding out about it. It
seemed that they would be sure to misuse this wonderful experience in some way: they wouldn't understand it; they'd
play around with it; they'd go off the beam with it! We know
now that of all the groups in the church, it is the young people

who are most wonderfully helped and blessed by the Baptism in the Holy Spirit, but we didn't know that *then*.

"Whatever you do," I had said to Jim, "don't talk to the teenagers about this." But now the word was out. Could we squelch it? Perhaps all was not lost. Susan was the daughter of my librarian, and her mother would understand. No problem there. Walter, I could probably keep under control. He worked at the church part-time, and I could keep an eye on him.

"That's okay, Jim," I said, thinking fast. "You send Sue home to her mother. I'll talk to Walter."

Sure enough, Susan's mother prayed with her, and she was joyfully baptized in the Holy Spirit. Walter—well, Walter was an example of someone who is filled with the Holy Ghost but not yet *baptized* in Him. He had an infilling all right! Did he ever! He floated around St. Mark's for a week in a happy cloud, "so heavenly-minded that he was no earthly good!" I knew he needed to "come through" completely to the Baptism in the Holy Spirit; the fullness of God that was in him had to find an outlet before it could be expressed effectively. So I invited him to the rectory.

"Come tonight at eight, and we'll pray. But don't tell any of the other kids!"

At eight o'clock, Walter was there, and we slipped into my study. It didn't take long to encourage him to begin praising God in new freedom. In the meantime, another drama was taking place. The first I knew of it was when Elberta showed up at the door of the study.

"You might just as well come up to the front room," she announced happily. "He's *there*, too!"

My wife had not been sharing in the fear I had felt about the young people, or about anything else, for that matter! She wasn't the kind to be too worried about what folks thought. She had found something wonderful from God, and she was enjoying it. Elberta had written a little about our experience to our daughter Margie, at college, and Margie told us later:

"When I got Mum's letter, Ellen and I (Ellen was her roommate, a Jewish girl) sat in bed and shook with excitement. Right away I wrote to my boyfriend and told him about it, too. He wrote back and said:

"When I got your letter, Margie, I was lying in bed in my dormitory just hating another guy in my class, and planning how I would like to get even with him; but as I read your letter, the hatred drained out of me, and I was filled instead with love. I jumped out of bed, and rushed downstairs into the common room to tell the other fellows!"

As I now followed Elberta into the living room, with Walter in my wake, I was stunned by what I saw. Over on the couch, laughing with joy, sat Margie and that same boyfriend. My daughter's chin was trembling as she was beginning to speak in tongues. The boyfriend had a a beatifically happy smile on his face. My older son, Stephen, was slumped down in a chair with his fist stuck in his mouth because, as he explained:

"I felt the new language coming up into my throat, but I was afraid I wouldn't get it right, so I didn't want to speak it out."

Conrad was sitting cross-legged on a hassock in the corner, laughing and crying at the same time. I looked at this little group and thought at first the kids were making fun. I said, rather angrily:

"This isn't a game!"

My wife replied:

"You're right, this is not a game: this is the Holy Spirit. Margie just asked me to tell them some more about the Baptism with the Holy Spirit," she continued, "and this is what happened."

The Spirit had fallen spontaneously on that little group of

young people, just as He had overwhelmed Susan and Walter with His love and power a few days earlier.

That night our daughter and her boyfriend and our younger son received the Holy Spirit, but our older son did not, for the simple reason that he wouldn't speak the language the Holy Spirit was providing. He held out that night and continued to hold out for several weeks; then one morning he came out of his bedroom with the announcement:

"Mum, I had a funny dream last night. I dreamed I had God locked up in my closet, and He was saying through the door, 'When are you going to let me out, Steve?'"

Very shortly after this, he "let God out," and began to speak in the Spirit. It was as though he had suddenly joined the family. We now had something in common that bridged the "generation gap." My fears about teenagers being too immature to be filled with God vanished.

How could something like this be kept from spreading among the other youngsters? It was obvious that something had happened to our kids. They were different. Their friends could see the change, and they asked questions. Susan and Walter tried to keep their counsel, but it was very difficult. There were other parents who had received the Holy Spirit, and wanted their teenagers to be blessed. Soon it was openly known that the young people were "catching it" too! Sadly enough, to the "opposition," the participation of the youth was regarded as further reason to try to put out the fire. The clouds had rolled in, and the storm was ready to break.

I believe that even at this point had I gone into the pulpit and told the people clearly what was happening, the rising tempest might well have died down. Unfortunately, I was, for the first time in my professional life, experiencing unpopularity. I had always avoided open argument and had been the great compromiser, and now I made the wrong move. I decided that if I

chose to be quiet — wrong decision

was very quiet about it all, and if the people involved were very quiet, too, those who were disturbed would calm down and the whole row would blow over.

Alas, I had reckoned without human nature! My silence on the subject and the quietness of the whole group simply darkened the suspicion that this was a dangerous, secret movement that would undermine the church and damage souls. I had also underestimated the irrepressible spread of the fire of the Holy Spirit, once it has been kindled. You can't keep Pentecost under wraps—it burns through!

8
The Storm Breaks

In spite of threatenings and rumours at home, the blessing continued to spread abroad. I had been enjoying the new freedom in the Lord for about three weeks when a call came from the Episcopal chaplain at one of the large universities in the Los Angeles area:

"I just have to talk to you, Dennis," he said. "I hardly know you, but I had an experience last night that's really shaken me up!" He proceeded to describe, almost point for point, an encounter with the Holy Spirit exactly like my own, including the fact that as he began to praise the Lord in the new language, he saw a vivid picture of Jesus on the Cross.

Another minister's life was touched, this time as a result of the Holy Spirit working through a child. Don and Shirley were among the first to be baptized in the Holy Spirit at St. Mark's. One day Shirley said to me:

"I've got something to tell you, Father Bennett. You know Chris, our six-year-old?"

I nodded.

"Well, the first part of this year we were baffled at what to do about him. He was the terror of the first grade! Not a day went by, it seemed, without our getting a call from the school that Chris had been sent to the office, or was in hot water of some kind. The teacher said he was just uncontrollable." She paused, and then looked at me with a twinkle in her eye. "Don and I had an idea what to do about it," she continued. "The Baptism in the Holy Spirit had helped us so tremendously, why shouldn't this experience help Chris?" Shirley saw the concern on my face and went on: "Now, don't get excited, Father Bennett. It's all right, honest it is! We sat Chris down and told him what had happened to us, and asked if he would like to have Jesus baptize him in the Holy Spirit. He said he would, so we prayed, and he began to speak in tongues almost immediately! He laughed happily and then ran off to play."

"Really, Shirley," I remonstrated, "this isn't a toy for children!"

"Listen to the rest of the story," she said firmly. "Several school days later, I got a phone call from Chris's teacher.

" 'What in the world has come over Chris?' she asked me. 'This week he's been my best pupil. He hasn't made any trouble at all, and he's so happy it's amazing!' I told her what had happened, and she said:

" 'I'll be right over. I need that too!' And do you know, Father Bennett, *she* came over and received the Holy Spirit!"

I was speechless as Shirley finished her story.

"And do you know who *she* is?" she asked me.

I shook my head.

"She's the wife of the assistant minister at one of the Lutheran churches! He's coming over to find out what it's all about too! We want you to be there to help us explain it all to him!"

The young minister was interested in his wife's experience. She had been a doubting Christian, almost an agnostic; so much so that the senior pastor and the leaders of the church had been questioning her fitness to be a pastor's wife. Her sudden acquisition of a truly radiant faith could not fail to impress them—and it all came about because of the change in one small child.*

While many such good things were taking place, the gulf of misunderstanding at the church continued to widen. My policy of "keep quiet and hope for the best" was definitely not working. The opposition was not directed at me personally, but the very small group of people who were stirring up the trouble were convinced that I had gone off the track, and that their mission was to bring me to my senses. For several months I tried to hold the church together by the compromise of silence on my part, but this simply gave the dissidents opportunity to work at sowing the seeds of discontent.

It was a strange time. I was upset by the growing attacks; yet I was enjoying God's blessings in a new dimension. Quite early in the game I had learned something of the peace of the Holy Spirit, and I learned it in a traffic jam! Our daughter was scheduled to come home from college in San Jose, California, for the Thanksgiving holiday, and the rest of the family was en route to the Los Angeles International Airport to meet her. It was a hot, sticky, and smoggy afternoon as we parked the car and walked toward the "Flight Arrivals" of the little local airline. I realized that ocean fog was rolling in to join forces with the smog, and that the airport was rapidly getting "socked in." An announcement over the public address system soon confirmed my fears; the flight had overflown Los Angeles because of the weather, and was on its way to Burbank.

We trudged back to the car. This time as we drove north the boulevard was jammed. The industrial plants that cluster

---

* This same Lutheran Church is now open to the charismatic renewal. The present pastor has received the baptism in the Holy Spirit, together with a number of members of the congregation.

around the airport were disgorging their workers, and traffic was bumper-to-bumper. The air was hotter than ever, with plenty of fresh exhaust fumes to add a little extra fillip to the smog, and it would be a good hour-and-a-half to Burbank! At the airport, I had elbowed my way to the ticket counter and pleaded with the harried attendant to ask that my daughter be paged when she arrived at Burbank and told to wait there for us. The airline clerk's preoccupied manner had not convinced me that he would remember to do it! Yet as we inched our way along, I was not tense. I wasn't gripping the wheel with sweaty palms, muttering exclamations of impatience under my breath, or giving opinions about the slowness and stupidity of the other drivers. I was singing—I caught myself at it!—singing a hymn! And I felt cool and calm, way down inside. I thought to myself:

I feel peaceful. I don't understand why.

Quick as a flash, the Holy Spirit said in my heart:

"Of course you don't. This is the peace that *passes* understanding!"

The next time I saw John and Joan, I said:

"You didn't tell me about 'the peace that passes understanding.' "

"Oh, did you just discover it?" John replied. He was as objective as if he and I had bought identical automobiles, and I had said to him:

"I didn't realize that the car would come equipped with air conditioning," and he had replied:

"Oh, did you just discover that on yours, too?"

We retrieved Margie safely from the Lockheed Air Terminal in Burbank and on the next day, Thanksgiving Day, I had the rare experience of sitting with my family in the congregation of my own church. One of my assisting ministers was conducting the service. As I listened to the familiar words of the Book of Common Prayer, and the reading of the Scripture lesson, I was suddenly overwhelmed by the beauty and significance of it. For the first time in my life, to my remembrance, I was moved to tears by a church service!

The Holy Spirit did not just enhance for me the worship of my own denomination, but He showed me the significance of others. A short time later I had my first experience of speaking to a group of Pentecostal ministers. (Six months earlier, I would have hesitated to address an assembly of Methodist or Presbyterians lest I compromise my Anglo-Catholic position!) I didn't know what to expect, although I had already found out that Pentecostals were very different from the "holy roller" caricature. I respected them because I knew from my research that these were the Christians who had preserved the understanding of the Baptism in the Holy Spirit, sometimes in the face of real persecution, and I owed them gratitude for the blessing that had come into my own life.

The setting of the meeting was unfamiliar, the form of worship was totally different from that used in the Episcopal Church, and the people were strangers to me; yet as they began to sing, and praise, and pray, I knew these were my brothers in the Lord, not because of any official connection, for we had none, but because I felt the wonderful thing the Scripture calls "the fellowship of the Holy Spirit."

My talk to the ministers was well-accepted, and I was amazed at the strength of the bond between us in the Lord. Few of these good men had what my church would consider adequate theological training, but I had more than an inkling that they were my superiors in the training that matters: knowing the Lord, and His ways.

After my testimony, one of the men on the platform asked permission to speak. As I listened, in my spirit I knew that the speaker was not sharing his own thoughts with us, but wisdom that God was giving:

"Father Bennett, we would love to have you join us, and there will always be a welcome for you in our churches, but we know that this is not the thing for you to do. You should stay in your own denomination so they can receive word of the Baptism in the Holy Spirit; for they will listen to you where they would not listen to us."

These words confirmed what I had already known in my heart, but it was surely the wisdom of God to underline the fact so well that day. Had He not, on the following day I might not have been quite so sure. That night as I knelt to say my prayers, my thoughts turned to the situation at the parish, which had been growing steadily more unbearable. I was burdened with a heavy load af anxiety and fear. I felt like a drinking glass into which had been poured two different liquids—light and heavy. The fire and joy of the Holy Spirit were there, undiminished, down in my heart, but they were overlaid and oppressed by fear and anxiety. My experience with the Pentecostal ministers, free, and rejoicing in the Holy Spirit, had stirred *my* spirit; and as I began my prayers, the joy of the Holy Spirit in me suddenly gained power and bubbled over in my new language. I could not stop praising God! I praised Him, and praised Him, and as I did so, I had an inner vision of the Almighty on His heavenly Throne, surrounded by hosts of creatures, earthly and heavenly, praising Him and glorifying Him! I could hardly stop praising! What was even more glorious was that the praise went on through my dreams, all night long.

God had prepared me well for what was coming the next day, Sunday, April 3. On that Passion Sunday, 1960, I did what I should have done five months before. The Holy Spirit had at last got the point through to me:

"I'm not asking you to hold this church together; I'm asking you to tell what has happened to you! This isn't your church anyway, it belongs to Jesus!"

I set aside the preaching schedule for the day, and went into the pulpit at the three morning services and simply shared what had happened to me. I appealed to the people to dismiss the ridiculous rumours.

The general reaction was open and tender—until the end of the second service. At that point my second assistant snatched off his vestments, threw them on the altar, and stalked out of the church crying:

"I can no longer work with this man!"

That "blew the lid off!" After the service concluded, outside on the patio, those who had set themselves to get rid of the movement of the Holy Spirit began to harangue the arriving and departing parishioners. One man stood on a chair shouting:

"Throw out the damn tongue-speakers!"

(Fortunately, even the most distressing events can have their humorous side. That morning, in the midst of the "tumult and the shouting," one little lady, at least, was blissfully unaware. As she shook hands with the greeter at the door she murmured: "It was a lovely service!")

The contrast was amazing: on the one hand was the unreasoning fury of the "opposition," while the people who had received the Baptism in the Holy Spirit were quietly moving around telling their story, faces shining with the love of God, and pleased somehow, in spite of the confusion, that at last they were free to witness openly.

As for me, I was appalled! This unexpected crisis was one too many! When one of my vestrymen, a leader of the "opposition," came to me and said bluntly: "You should resign!" I was ready to do so.

I am often asked the question: "Why didn't you hang on

and fight it out?" It is true, I didn't *have* to leave, for there is no way to force an Episcopal rector to resign against his will as long as he is not guilty of any moral or canonical offence, and even then he is entitled to a trial, but I was tired of being on the spot. I knew that the little group that had arrayed themselves against me would fight me to the death; that it could easily turn into a court battle, with much unfortunate publicity. It didn't seem to be the best way to proclaim the Good News!

Then, too, I had a strong need to "think it over." A lot had happened to me in a fairly short space of time, and I did not feel that I completely understood it all. If I had the knowledge and background on the whole matter that I have now, things might have been different, but I didn't. I wanted to take inventory, to sit down quietly somewhere and think, and pray about it.

So it was with relief that I said to the vestryman:

"Okay, I'll resign. Right away." At the 11.00 a.m. service, I announced my resignation to an astonished and distressed congregation and walked away from the parish that I had served for seven years.

When I came home that memorable Passion Sunday I found my wife waiting for me, her eyes shining!

"Dennis," she said, "it was wonderful! We got to tell so many people what was really happening!" I didn't at that moment share her enthusiasm; I was still too shocked by the morning's events, but later I began to realize the truth of her words. The phone and the doorbell began to ring, as people came by to ask the question:

"What is it all about?"

We suddenly found ourselves free to talk.

That night there was a real air of impending victory when seventy-five enthusiastic Christians met for prayer and praise. They felt that if enough people at the church received the power of the Holy Spirit, and found how beneficial it is, the parish might yet be united. Many people from St. Mark's and elsewhere came, and many were baptized in the Holy Spirit.

Contrary to popular report, there was no "split" at St. Mark's. The "opposition" group was actually very small. The majority of the church had no idea "what had hit them." My only dispute with those who created the furor at St. Mark's was that they really did not investigate carefully, but rather acted from prejudice and hearsay—a very human thing to do, indeed!

I didn't know what to do next, but just tried to follow the Lord one step at a time. God continued to do great things.

Louise, who was eighty-three years old, for ten years had been suffering from a painful arthritis of the spine, and angina of the heart. She was forced to keep to her bed most of the time, and I had often called at her little home.

Louise had friends who had received the Holy Spirit, and one day, shortly after the blow-up at St. Mark's she said to me:

"I believe all this that is happening is real, and I know, too, that if you lay your hands on me, Father Bennett, I will be healed!"

Accordingly I laid my hands on her head, and asked God to heal her. I do not remember that I personally felt much confidence, in fact I left the room after praying for her without even asking if she felt any better! About a week later when I saw her at a prayer meeting, I said:

"How are you, Louise?"

She replied: "I'm fine, *of course*!"

Later that week she came to our house and *skipped* around the front room.

"See what I can do!" she chortled.

A year after her healing she wrote me a note saying that she was still feeling just fine. She added that one evening her neighbour, seventy-two years of age, had locked herself out of her house.

"She's a bit crippled up," Louise said, "so *I* climbed in the window and let her in! I do get a bit tired sometimes," she added.

Three weeks after my resignation, on April 25, the traditional feast of St. Mark, it seemed fitting that those of us who had been meeting together regularly for prayer should fast and pray for the parish and its future. At the end of the day we all met at the rectory and began by reading the evening lessons from the Prayer Book.

"Oh," I said, as I looked in the lectionary (the list of daily Bible readings in the front of the Prayer Book), "the Old Testament lesson is from the Apocrypha.* I don't have a copy of the Apocrypha here, so I'll pick another reading instead."

"Can't you get an Apocrypha from your office?" inquired one of the women. "I think we ought to read the lessons as they are appointed. It seems important somehow."

I found an Apocrypha and turned to the evening lesson. It was from Ecclesiasticus 51 : 13–22. Everyone listened dutifully as I read the first part of the lesson which was a typical piece

---

* The Apocrypha is a collection of fourteen books, written in the time between the Old and New Testaments. Some of them are historical, some are prophetic, some collections of proverbs and wisdom, one or two illustrative stories, and one very beautiful long psalm. Much of the Apocrypha is very helpful, and any Christian would benefit from reading it. The books were not accepted as a part of the Canonical Scripture in the early days. Rome made them a part of her official Scriptures at the Council of Trent between 1545 and 1563. The Episcopal Church, following the custom of the Church of England, reads them: "For example of life and instruction of manner; but yet doth it not apply them to establish any doctrine . . ." (Article of Religion VI)). Nevertheless, selections from the Apocrypha are appointed to be read on certain days at Morning and Evening Prayer.

of "wisdom" literature, poetic, but not too exciting. I read the twenty-first verse:

"My heart was troubled in seeking her (wisdom): therefore have I got a good possession." Then as I read the twenty-second verse there was sensation:

"The Lord hath given me a tongue for my reward, and I will praise Him therewith!"

How could the Holy Spirit have known and guided the compilers of that lectionary, many years before, to select a lesson for St. Mark's Day that would come through with such meaning to this little group of Christians? Marvellous are the ways of God! In amazement we began to praise Him.

Many spiritually hungry people came to talk about and pray for the power of the Holy Spirit which would enable them to live more effective Christian lives. We met in private homes. Since I was no longer rector of the parish, as an Episcopal priest I would have been violating canon law had I held public meetings; the authorities interpreted our actions as uncanonical anyway. It was soon clear that if I continued, I might not be able to remain in the Episcopal ministry. I could not forget the words of wisdom from the minister at the Pentecostal rally, that I was needed in my own denomination.

We wrestled with various thoughts of what to do next. I began to investigate what other leaders of the Episcopal Church thought about this renewing experience of our faith. Madelyn, the church librarian, was an old friend of the then presiding bishop of the Episcopol Church, the late Bishop Lichtenberger. At her urging, he invited me to come and talk with him. I flew to San Antonio, Texas, and unfolded my story. I must have talked for more than an hour while he listened patiently and attentively and with obvious interest. When I finished he said:

"Dennis, there's nothing wrong with this. It's wonderful,

but you know I don't have any authority to help you with your local situation."

Even so, his interest and kindness encouraged me to carry my investigation further. Later in the month a priest of the diocese, a friend of mine who had been quite interested in what was going on in my life, returned from a conference in the San Francisco area and said to me:

"You know, Dennis, I shared your story with the bishops from Seattle and Portland, and they are not closed to your experience. Why don't you go and see them?"

I determined to do just that. I had had some contact with both of these men before and when I wrote them, each said he would be happy to talk with me.

9
Fire Moves North

It was a lovely June day when the 720 Boeing jet in which I was a passenger taxied out to the end of Los Angeles International's runway 25-R and swung into her take-off roll. It was not quite so nice as she touched down on runway 16 at Seattle-Tacoma, after a tolerably "hairy" approach through a low overcast. The son of a good friend in Van Nuys, stationed in Seattle in the Army, met me at the airport and took me into town. As we rode along Highway 99 in Jon's little Corvette, through the congested Boeing plant traffic (the freeway has relieved this picture since then), I had my introduction to the "Queen City" of Seattle. Especially in those days, the visitor coming from the airport did not get the best impression at first view.

"It's a beautiful city, but you'd sure never know it on a day like this, or in this part of town," said Jon; and indeed, as we drove through the grimy industrial area and on into town under lowering skies, my own feelings were more than a little clouded.

However, the next day dawned bright and cheerful, and my spirit was much higher as I walked into the diocesan house to keep a ten o'clock appointment with the bishop. I was ushered into a sunny, high-windowed room, which commanded a wonderful view of the city and its environs to the west. Right below lay Lake Union, busy with small boats and variegated shipping, including four old clipper ships riding at anchor. In the middle distance, beyond the town, Puget Sound sparkled blue and inviting, dotted with green islands, while on the horizon the snowy Olympics were rifting through into the sunshine. It was indeed a beautiful day, and as Jon had said, a beautiful place.

"Why, good morning, Dennis!"

My eyes and thoughts returned to the office, as I stood to greet the man I had come so far to see. The Rt. Rev. William Fisher Lewis, Bishop of Olympia, was an old acquaintance. He beamed at me happily and motioned me to sit down.

"Tell me about it," he invited, leaning back in his chair, "I've heard a little. I was in Los Angeles when the excitement took place at St. Mark's. What's it all about?"

As simply as I could, I told him my story.

"There's nothing wrong with that," he stated firmly, as I concluded. "Look, Dennis, what about coming up to this diocese? Bring the fire with you! I don't have a big church to offer you, but I do have a little mission out in the Ballard area, St. Luke's. It's never quite got "off the ground" in the last sixty years. I've got to do something or close it up. Would you like to go out and look over the situation?"

I was interested in his offer and I knew I'd like to work under the leadership of this man. I was even more sure of it when he said:

"First, let's pray," and suiting the action to the word, he knelt. I joined him and together we asked the guidance of God. I was to learn that I would never leave Bishop Lewis's office without kneeling and praying with him.

Today, the Ballard district of Seattle has undergone a "face-lifting". Sharp-looking new apartments and business houses have sprung up. A large marina, with its associated restaurants and concessions, has brought new life to the area, while the Seattle World's Fair occasioned the making of the rough Shilshole Waterfront into a park; but ten years ago, and especially for a person used to the bright artificiality of Los Angeles, Ballard seemed a gloomy place.

The outside of the little church building was shabby, and the surrounding residences were quite old and some were run-down. This wasn't the kind of thing I had been used to for the last seven years! However, when I went inside, my feelings changed. It was warm and attractive, neat and clean, and had that feeling of having been "prayed in". Obviously, *somebody* cared about "St. Luke's, Ballard". I turned to the archdeacon of the diocese who had brought me.

He smiled: "It's not bad, is it?" I nodded my agreement as we walked down the steps to his car.

"Not bad at all."

Heading southward and homeward, I stopped at Portland, Oregon, for a chat with Bishop Carman. Again I was received most cordially and again I told my story to an interested listener. When I finished, the Bishop made one terse comment:

"This is where the Pentecostals get their fire, isn't it?"

He, too, invited me to come to his diocese, but somehow I felt that my new direction would be that little run-down church in Seattle, Washington.

Back in Van Nuys, Elberta and I talked and prayed, and arrived at our decision: we would go to St. Luke's in Seattle. I know that my decision was made for mixed reasons: first, God did seem to be opening the way; second, I was eager to see what would happen if the Baptism in the Holy Spirit was openly accepted and taught in a local congregation; third, I did not want to leave the security of my own denomination; and last but not least, I was tired of being "on the spot," and wanted to get away! How gracious God is to use a mixed bag of motives like that!

The next week, the Assemblies of God of Southern California were holding their annual men's fellowship retreat in the mountains at Pinecrest, and I was invited to be the speaker. I was growing quite accustomed to my Pentecostal brothers and their ways and I knew I could expect an inspiring time. Naturally, one thought was uppermost in my mind: had I done the right thing in deciding to go to Seattle? As I sat on the platform looking out at five hundred or more men worshipping and praising God, I said a prayer in my heart:

"Oh, Lord, I need confirmation that my decision was the right one." I had hardly formed the prayer in my thoughts before a man whom I had never seen before stood up and began to speak in a language given by the Holy Spirit. As soon as he stopped, another man I had never seen began to interpret, and this was the essence of it:

"If you will go with Me and not deny the work of My Holy Spirit, I will prosper your ministry!"

I said quietly: "Thank You, Lord!"

In the meantime, publicity guns were firing; I found myself both famous and notorious. I didn't mind being considered a hero, but didn't care too much for the role of villain! After all, up until the explosion of St. Mark's, I had always been the "fair-haired boy" who got along with everyone. A "successful" minister is usually a "hail-fellow-well met": a "nice guy," everyone's friend. Now I suddenly found myself a controversial figure, and didn't quite like it! Hearing that *Newsweek* *

* *Newsweek*, July 4, 1960, page 77.

magazine was preparing an article scheduled to appear the first of July, I said to Elberta:

"Will you stay here and pack up the house? I'm going to head for Seattle right away. I can't stand any more phone calls, and when that magazine article comes out, it'll be insufferable!"

I meant it too, and my wife, quietly enduring my cowardice, would have done it, but I had no more than declared my intention when the telephone rang. With a gesture of impatience I reached for the instrument:

"Father Bennett?"

"Speaking."

"This is ———." The caller gave the name of a well-known commentator in the Los Angeles area. "I want to do a story on the things that are happening at St. Mark's; you know, speaking in tongues, and all that."

"I'm sorry," I said, "but I'm just getting ready to leave for Seattle, and won't have time."

"Well, okay," the commentator said, "but I'm going to do the broadcast whether to co-operate or not." His voice rather indicated he thought he was dealing with a bunch of happy "kooks" and was anticipating some laughs. I felt that I had to stay in town after all, if only to defend myself! We set up an appointment for the next day. Thank heavens it was radio and not *television*!

The next morning we were in the midst of packing when the doorbell rang.

"Oh, that must be the radio interviewer now," I said to Don and Shirley, two friends from St. Mark's whom we had asked to take part in the programme with us.

Don looked out the window and exclaimed, "Oh, no! Cameramen!" It *was* TV!

My wife and I glanced at one another aghast over the stacks

of cartons that nearly filled our front room. In came the well-known commentator, a breezy little man with an unmistakable air of "show biz" about him and of wanting to get the whole silly thing over with as soon as possible. He was visibly surprised as he met the four of us. Apparently we weren't as "kooky" as he had expected. His manner changed as we talked together. He asked many questions and became increasingly interested, more and more showing that he realized that this was not just a game, but very serious business. He seemed sincere, and when he sat down with me to decide how the interview should be set up, he asked: "About this 'speaking in tongues'—would you be willing to do it for me now?" I agreed and prayed briefly "in the Spirit."

He was visibly moved as he remarked: "Father Bennett, you've got to do this on the programme as part of the interview! If you don't, the audience will still think it's something crazy, but if they hear you speak, they'll know that it's for real."

Before the interviewer had arrived, the others and I had resolved not to speak in tongues over the air; we were sure that this would be asked of us. Nevertheless, I knew that he was right, and so it came about that I did pray in the Spirit, speaking in tongues on TV in the sight and sound of what may well have been a milion Los Angelenes. The programme was sensitively handled, and an effective witness was made to God's work. The *Newsweek* article came out, and we survived that, too. The next week found us on our way to Seattle, and on Sunday, July 15, I conducted my first service in St. Luke's, Ballard.

A good-sized group of people had turned out to meet and to hear the new minister. My first sermon was simply aimed at letting them know that I was "normal"! I liked them, and they seemed to respond to me, although I myself was in much fear and trepidation. I had just had a church blow up in my face, and the experience was not one I wanted to repeat.

But I soon began to discover the real discouragement that there was at St Luke's. The very first week, Wally, a young businessman, came to me:

"I hate to do this to you when you've just arrived, Father Bennett," he said, "but I'm going to have to resign as Sunday School Superintendent. I just don't have anything left to give. I seem to have lost whatever faith I had, after all that we have been through around here." With this, he handed me his keys and books.

Ballard, lovingly nicknamed "herring-bone hill," had originally been a Scandinavian fishing village on the shores of Puget Sound, and it is not hard to understand the struggles of an Episcopal Church to get started, as the early religious colour of the community was almost entirely Lutheran. However, in recent years the population of the district had increased to around 100,000, only a minority of whom were Scandinavian, and yet St. Luke's, the only Episcopal Church in the area, had never managed to get on its feet.

Like so many struggling missions, St. Luke's had run the gamut in leadership: young men on the way up, willing to stay until economic pressure or ambition forced them to accept what one of my seminary professors called a "louder call"; older men nearing retirement, bringing the ripeness and wisdom of years, but looking for a lighter work load, and unable or unwilling to meet the challenge; and, most difficult of all, men who were hampered by some personal problem in their lives, or in their families. St. Luke's had enjoyed some very good leadership from time to time, and some good foundations had been laid, especially by one young man whom they had liked very much and who had stayed five years. But by the time I came, the bishop was ready to close the church—he had the padlock in his hand. I was the last chance! Some of the people told me later:

"Boy, when we heard the bishop was sending *you*, we wondered what kind of last chance we were being given! We had read about you in the papers!"

The first few weeks in Seattle were uneventful. The sheer natural magnificence of the country took my breath away. We had arrived during one of those spells of clear summer weather which northwesterners sometimes enjoy, and which, when they come, more than make up for a lot of rainy days! On every hand there were snow-clad mountains: to the west the beautiful line of the Olympics, and to the east the alpine ruggedness of the Cascades. There was blue water and green forests and —fresh air! In these surroundings, I began to enjoy the idea of settling down to a routine pastorate for a while. I wanted to be once again a nicely accepted, quiet, respectable parish priest! On the other hand, I had seen God's power in action among His people, and I knew very well I could not long be content to lead a congregation without telling them about receiving the Holy Spirit.

Nevertheless, I was mighty hesitant about beginning, but just as I was making myself comfortable, there came another blast. In August, *Time* magazine devoted a full page to the Van Nuys incident and finished by saying that I had come to St. Luke's, Seattle.* The people came that Sunday literally waving the magazine over their heads:

"We're internationally famous!" they cried. "But *what* is it all about?"

That morning, again smoked out of hiding, I told my story. I concluded:

* *Time*, August 15, 1960, pp. 53–55.

"I'm not going to push this on you at all. If you want to know more about it, you'll have to ask me; then I'll be perfectly happy to talk to you about it—I'll talk all night, if necessary!"

10

Off the Runway

"Whew! Thank goodness we're finally getting settled!" said Elberta, plunking herself down on the settee in the front room of our new home in Seattle.

It was a nice little house: big enough for our family, yet small enough to be cared for easily. Its one dramatic feature was that out of the south living-room window one had a perfectly framed view of Mt. Rainier when he had a mind to be seen! (Rainier broods over Seattle like an American Fujiyama, all 14,410 feet of him, showing that fascinating characteristic of mountains to look close or far away, huge or quite insignificant, according to the location of the viewer. I have seen Rainier when he seemed to fall back and become just a distant peak on a far skyline, much farther away than his actual distance of sixty miles.)

A knock came at the door, and we welcomed two of our new parishioners.

"Just thought we'd stop by to see how you were doing, and if we could help you," said Alice.

We chatted about this and that, but eventually they came to the point:

"What you were talking about on Sunday in your sermon," said Jack, "—we're interested. Would you consider coming to our house on Friday night? We have one or two others who are interested, too."

When Friday evening came, Elberta and I were surprised to see nine people waiting for us. Four men and five women looked at us expectantly as we took our seats in the living room. As we sat and talked, and imbibed tea and cake, I sized up the group. Most I had met before, or seen in church; one or two I did not recall. Their occupations, it turned out, were various. One was a pharmacist, another a personnel man for Boeing aviation. There were two in insurance work, and our host worked in the shipping room of the Seattle *Times*. Of the women, two were employed: one as a secretary, and the other as a research technician at the University of Washington Medical School.

They were all "old-timers" at St. Luke's. This was emphatically not a group of new disciples gathered from among the "fringe"; this was part of the little nucleus who had worked and struggled through the years to keep the church alive. Most of them had held, or were holding, positions of responsibility in the congregation. Several were, or had been, on the vestry, the official board of the church. I was surprised and delighted to see among them the young man, Wally, who had just resigned as Sunday School Superintendent because he was so discouraged. It was interesting too, as they told me later, that these people had not been close friends. Each seemed to have been moved separately to come that night; they had not urged one another, and each couple seemed somewhat surprised to see the others there.

"Start at the beginning," said our host, Jack. "What happened down there in Southern California?"

I talked for nearly two hours while my listeners sat in rapt attention. When I stopped, there was a moment or two of silence, broken by one of the men:

"So there is more to this Christianity than we've realized!"

"We ought to go on and talk about this all night!" said someone else. We agreed to meet the following Friday at the home of one of the other couples, and the next week all were on hand, including the husband who had been working and unable to attend the first gathering. As we took our places, someone said:

"Tonight we don't want to talk, we want to pray!"

This comment shook me a little, for these people were not the "prayer-group" type, nor did they come from "prayer-meeting" backgrounds. They were, rather, typical Episcopalians: earnest, down-to-earth people who felt the need of religious observance, but who had been taught not to get too excited about it. Religion was a "department" of their lives, wonderful in its place, but not too much related to their other activities.

Why didn't I, then and there, pray for these open and eager people to be baptized in the Holy Spirit? Simple enough—I was afraid to! I knew what was likely to happen as soon as folks began to get "fired-up." I remembered, only too well, that vestryman's "Praise the Lord" at the coffee hour at St. Mark's the year before!

The prayer meeting that night would have seemed undramatic enough to anyone who did not know how unusual it was for it to happen at all! Everyone agreed with enthusiasm that we should meet again on the following Friday, and we also concurred that we should move to the church parish hall. This move would forestall any foolish rumours that might get started if we kept on meeting in private homes. At the church, we would be in a public place where all the world was free to come and see, if it chose.

A somewhat expanded group met on that third Friday night. With us was our pretty, twenty-year-old daughter, Margaret, who had joined us in Seattle that week. (She had remained in California when we left, in order to finish her year at college.) Also present was Jim, the man who had been my youngest assistant at Van Nuys, who, with his wife Sharon, was visiting in the area. Jim and Sharon were an engaging young couple and gladly shared with our Seattle-ites something of their own experience in the Holy Spirit. So did Margie. We prayed around the room that night and as we prayed, the Presence of the Lord was so strong that several of the group were moved to tears.

It was the custom of the Bishop of Olympia to call together the clergy of his diocese for a conference once a year, and the following week was the time of this conference. As I and my fellow ministers arrived at the little Oregon seacoast resort where we were to spend three days, there was a holiday spirit of good fellowship. The programme for the first evening got under way: evening prayer, supper, a lecture by the guest—a very austere and scholarly English bishop!—and the session closed with the nightly prayer office of compline. We fragmented off in various directions: some to bed, some for a late stroll on the beach, but most to get together in various rooms for talk—reminiscences, anecdotes, and some good solid gossip about church matters and personalities, especially bishops! Five or six of my new acquaintances among the clergy centred in on me and said:

"We want to hear about your experience."

One fellow offered his room, and we were soon deep into the story. I don't know what they were expecting to hear, but all of them listened most intently to everything that I had to say, questioning me until well after midnight. I looked at my watch and exclaimed:

"Say, you guys, it's nearly one o'clock! We've got to go to bed!"

There was a pause. Nobody made a move to go. Then from one crewcut young priest, sitting on the floor, came:

"We ought to pray."

This suggestion startled me. Episcopal clergy certainly pray, but their praying tends to be either a private matter, or liturgical "common" prayer. It was quite unusual for this young man to suggest an informal group prayer, and even more unusual when in a very relaxed way these men proceeded to pray —good prayers, spontaneous prayers.

Another day went by, with lectures, discussion, prayer, and fellowship, and the next night after compline again a group came to me with the request:

"Let's go and talk about your experience, Dennis."

Some of the men were repeaters from the night before, but most were new. Again we talked, and again, in the wee small hours of the morning, somebody who had not been present the night before said:

"We ought to pray!" And we prayed.

The third night it was the archdeacon of the diocese, the man who had taken me out to see St. Luke's Church on my first visit to Seattle, who said:

"Dennis, I haven't heard your whole story. Won't you come to my room tonight?"

The archdeacon was much beloved and respected, and when I entered his room, there were fourteen men waiting. Again I talked of what had happened to me, and again when I finished there were many questions. Then came the pause I was almost expecting by now, and someone said:

"Let's pray!"

What followed was really very strange. As those men prayed, they sounded like a Pentecostal meeting! One said: "Praise the Lord!"; another, "Hallelujah!" Suddenly one of the priests, a man I did not know, jumped to his feet and began to recite the "Sanctus":

"Holy, Holy, Holy, Lord God of Sabaoth; heaven and earth are full of the majesty of Thy Glory." His face was radiant, and his hands lifted. Suddenly he began to prophesy. Beautiful words of promise and blessing came from his lips. There was no missing the fact that these words were inspired of God. He ended, and fell into his chair, a look of sheer amazement on his face.

"Where in the world did *that* come from?" he gasped.

On the final morning of the conference, as I was preparing to leave, someone behind me asked:

"Would you like to ride home with us?"

I turned around and was scarcely sure I recognized the young minister who had spoken to me. I had met him and conversed with him when he had first arrived at the conference. He had told me how frustrated and empty his life had become, and how he was thinking very seriously of leaving the ministry. Certainly I had rarely seen anyone look more unhappy. Subsequently, he had been present at all three of the informal, late-night meetings. Plainly something had already happened to him, for his face was as happy and smiling now as it had been sad and gloomy before. I accepted his invitation with pleasure. As we drove back to Seattle, every few miles he slapped his knee exclaiming:

"Praise God!"

When we arrived at my home, Elberta was waiting with interesting news:

"Dennis, guess what! Father W. is in town—you know, the man who wrote you from Illinois! He has some free time, and would like to come over and visit us!"

I was delighted. Father W. was the Rector of a good-sized

parish in the Chicago area. Right in the midst of my troubles in Van Nuys, he had written to me to tell me that they had been experiencing the Baptism in the Holy Spirit in his parish for the past five years.

"Most of my key people have received, and it's wonderful the way God's love and joy is being shown in their lives," he wrote. And he proceeded to encourage me to stand my ground. I was very pleased, of course, for up until this time, as an Episcopal priest, I had felt very alone in my experience. I had telephoned him and we had had much exchange of correspondence. Now here he was in Seattle!

I called him immediately and he agreed to meet with us that evening. I quickly telephoned all the little Friday group. Would they like to meet another Episcopal priest who believed in the Baptism with the Holy Spirit? Would they? Can a fish swim?! They were all at our home in very short order, plus some old friends from Van Nuys who were visiting—the neuro-surgeon, "Duke", and his wife, Claire—and the once de-pressed and now joyful young minister, who had brought me home from the conference and stayed to see what further blessing God had in store for *him*!

Father W. from Chicago turned out to be a personable man in early middle-life. His pleasant manner and openness quickly broke the ice, and he was soon telling of his own experience and how people in his congregation had been blessed. Then he looked at those present:

"Is there anyone here who would like to receive the Holy Spirit?" he asked.

This was the question I had been avoiding, or postponing. I was sitting on the couch, but I felt much as I did when I was about to solo an airplane for the first time. Sitting securely on the runway, you have no problems, but neither are you getting anywhere! You must apply full power to take off, and *then* you have your hands full! This man was about to push in the throttle for me! I knew that the minute we invited God to apply His power to this group of Christians we would "take off" and begin to go places, but I was the pilot—could I fly the ship without mishap this time? That had been a wild ride down in Van Nuys! Was I ready for another?

In the last nine years I have had many church leaders say to me in one way or another, "Dennis, we know that the church organization is dying and that we need something to help us. What you are talking about might be what we need, but, oh, Dennis, we just can't afford to have any *trouble*!" I, as an administrator, knew what they meant. If the boat is floating, even though it is gunwale deep in the water, and the waves are sloshing over the decks, for heaven's sake don't rock it! What I failed to realize was that St. Luke's was already resting quietly on the bottom of the lake, and there was no fear of rocking the boat. Rather, the attitude was, "If you think you can raise her—go ahead and try!"

Father W. looked at his watch:

"Don't have to leave for the airport for an hour-and-a-half," he smiled happily. "That will be plenty of time for everyone here to be baptized with the Holy Spirit."

I sat firmly on the couch—*This I've got to see!*

The little contingent of Episcopalians needed no urging: they were ready. So was the young priest who had brought me home. I watched as my friend from Chicago laid hands on these people. One after another they were prayed for, and repeatedly and simply we saw and heard the miracle of Pentecost re-enacted. "They were all filled with the Holy Ghost, and began to speak in new languages, as the Spirit gave them utterance." [1]

Father W. quietly and simply encouraged them to open their mouths and begin to speak "as the Spirit gave them utterance." No such encouragement was needed for the young priest from the clergy conference! Before Father W. came anywhere near him, he threw back his head and began to speak fluently in a new language, while a glorious radiance overspread his already glowing countenance. With some of the others, it was almost as spontaneous, while some needed a little help to overcome their shyness. These good folk who had struggled so many years to do something for God in Ballard were suddenly aware of His power and glory in them in a new way.

It was impossible to miss the change that was visibly taking place. Joy, freedom, and spiritual understanding came as the new language poured from their lips. Though our visitor had to leave, the work had begun. Father W. had not imparted the Power, nor would the Power leave when he left. He had simply showed these people how to accept and express That which was already in them because they were in Christ. They were fulfilling the prayer which had been said for them at confirmation —that they might "increase in Thy Holy Spirit more and more . . ."* We were off the runway and "climbing out"—but what next? I was braced!

There was one interesting sidelight on this evening's experience: Jack, the member of the group in whose home we had first met, was an ardent bowler and had had to bowl in a tournament, so arrived late at the vicarage. He told us:

"When I came up the road, I saw the light outside your house, Father Bennett, and it was shining many times brighter than a one-hundred watt light *could* shine! I knew that I must hurry when I saw that because surely something wonderful was going on!"

* Not that the Holy Spirit would increase in *them*, which is the way we tend to think of the situation, but that *they* would increase in the Holy Spirit, that is, make more of themselves available to Him.

II
Airborne

The next afternoon I received a telephone call.

It was Pat, one of the group who had received the Holy Spirit the night before.

"I don't understand all that happened to me at the meeting last night," she said, hesitantly, "but I've been getting some words all day long, and I think they're for you. Can I have an appointment to tell you about them sometime?"

"If you've got some words from the Lord," I said, "I know better than to keep *Him* waiting. Come on over!"

She arrived at the office.

"The Lord seems to want me to say this," she began, seating herself across the room: "'You are afraid. You are afraid that this church will blow up like the church in Van Nuys! But don't be afraid. You'll never have any trouble here that you can't handle, and you'll have strong support from the top down!'"

As she spoke, I could have no doubt whatever that the Lord was using her as His messenger on that day. She could not possibly have known how much those words were true, and were needed. I had indeed been living with fear much of the time since the explosion in Van Nuys. I had not realized how oppressed I was until suddenly the oppression was broken. It seemed that I could feel the hot wind of the Holy Spirit blowing in my face, and that a silver rain of joy was visibly coming down from heaven! My heart began to leap with joy—I laughed, I shouted, I praised God! I am afraid I startled the newly-baptized-in-the-Holy Spirit Christian whom God had used as His emissary.

With this kind of assurance from the Holy Spirit, I plunged into the new work with enthusiasm. "The most important thing is to get started visiting people," I had said to Florence, the church secretary who had been heroically holding things together at St. Luke's while they were without a minister. "I'm going to divide the community into areas, and appoint a 'key family' over each area. We've got to get *organized*!"

In the very first St. Luke's newsletter after our arrival, I was all set to get "churchy."

"Just as soon as we are settled and moved in, I intend to begin an intensive round of visiting," I had written. Brave words! I thought *I* knew what to do about St. Luke's. I had revived a couple of other dead little churches in my time, and calling or visiting was basic. Ministers are trained to pay calls on people, in the hopes that people will come and "pay a call" on God! But clearly, God had other ideas. *He* was going to revive this church. St. Luke's was going to be different; it wasn't going to be a group of dependent souls being "taken care of" by a minister. These people were going to be equipped to help each other, and those around them, too. I was never permitted to carry out my "calling programme." God did allow me to care for the people who were in real need—sick or in trouble—but He never let me organize a round of home visiting for public relations purposes.

I have often been told:

"The reason for the revival at St. Luke's Church is that you are a clever organizer who knows just how to go about the business of building up a congregation!" The fact is that my "cleverness," if any, was not allowed to be used. All the little tricks of the trade that I had acquired in sixteen years of ministry were never put to use, because God kept me too busy to use them!

It had been only our second week in Seattle when the pastor of a nearby Assembly of God Church came to see me.

"Would you come and tell us of your experience, Dennis?" he said. That was the first of many invitations, so many that I soon saw that I would have to limit my acceptances. During the first four months as vicar of St. Luke's, I travelled to Denver, Spokane, Portland, and Vancouver, B.C., as well as to many nearby communities and local churches to tell the story. I began to be asked to speak to groups of ministers and lay people of many denominations: Methodist, Baptist, Quaker, and Lutheran were some of the first invitations. Lay people and pastors of all these groups, and many others, began to receive the Holy Spirit. My own bishop asked me to speak at the Clericus, the meeting of the local clergy of the Episcopal Church, where I was received with courtesy and interest. Several more Episcopal priests were at this time baptized in the Holy Spirit.

In the newsletter from January 8, 1961, appears the first of many similar statements:

"I am trying to hold these outside engagements to a minimum!"

It soon became evident to me, and to the people of St. Luke's that these "outside engagements" were to be a large part of my ministry, for I was one of the few ministers from an "old-line" denomination who was "willing and able" to talk about my experience of the Baptism in the Holy Spirit. Moreover, my background and academic training equipped me to explain the work of the Holy Spirit in a manner acceptable to the "intellectuals" and to fellow ministers. As for the people of St. Luke's Church, from the beginning they accepted my dual role with patience and understanding, and in doing so, felt that they had a part in an outreach ministry.

I was able to be away from the parish frequently because the laypeople were taking their rightful place as ministers and priests to God and to one another. When I was away, "business" continued as usual, for the newly-empowered-by-the-Holy-Spirit people, because of their new desire to serve, were only too willing to lead meetings, pray with people, conduct services, and even preach sermons in church on Sunday, and do it all very effectively! When I returned from an outside engagement they would often say to me:

"We had a wonderful time while you were away, Father Bennett!"

I found, too, that the finances of the church did not falter when I was away. I was becoming a commanding officer leading an army made up of soldiers who were capable of doing their own fighting, rather than a purveyor of spiritual remedies to a lot of dependent customers! It was great!

The first "fired-up" St. Lukans of course were telling their experiences to their friends. We began to meet regularly on Friday nights at the church, and there, as I gave my witness, I was joined by others with a story to tell.

"Guess what happened last night?" Amy's face was positively shining with joy. "We had some old friends over to our house and they accepted Jesus!"

I would hardly have known it was the same person that I had spotted in the congregation one Sunday morning shortly after my arrival in Seattle.

Good heavens, that woman looks depressed! I had thought. I learned that the woman's name was Amy, and that she had a husband, Ed, who occasionally came to church—when he wasn't fishing! Somewhat to my surprise, Amy had stopped me after church one fine Sunday morning:

"I hear you are having some prayer meetings in people's homes," she said. "Why don't you come and have one in ours?" Accordingly, several evenings later we did. As people were assembling, Amy said:

"I have a bad sore throat. Would you pray for me, Father Bennett?" Calling a man to help who had already been remarkably used in praying for the sick, we laid hands on Amy's head and the soreness immediately left her throat. But that wasn't all! The Lord also baptized her in the Holy Spirit, and she began to speak in tongues!

How things changed for that couple! When Ed saw what happened to Amy, he said:

"I want that, too!" We prayed for him. He had a hard time beginning to speak in tongues, because he was a bit shy and inhibited. Obviously, the Holy Spirit was at work in him, and as at so many other times I was tempted to say:

"Oh, well, that's all right. Never mind about the 'tongues.' They'll probably come later." But God again made Himself clear on the subject. It wasn't long before Ed reported:

"I'm beginning to speak in tongues in my dreams at night!" After that, it was just a matter of time until he was speaking fluently in his waking hours, and at will. (Since then we have known of many cases in which "speaking in tongues" came first in a dream.) Once again I had opportunity to see how completely the blessing of Pentecost could change two people. Both Ed and Amy had "church" backgrounds. Ed had given up on expecting anything important to happen at "church." Amy was hanging on, as women in a family often do. When Ed saw *evidence* his wife healed and suddenly brought to a glowing life in the Holy Spirit, he immediately wanted to share in something so obviously good.

Now instead of Amy being in church looking bored, with Ed away fishing, Amy and Ed were in church not only every Sunday, but several times on Sunday, and also at meetings several times during the week. They had "come alive" in the Spirit.

They said: "You know, before we were baptized in the Holy Spirit our only concern was to get through the weekend! We would have some friends over for a visit, but it was usually pretty dull. A few drinks would help to liven things up, but not much. Now we get our friends over and tell them about Jesus! It's much more exciting."

It wasn't just what was said that moved people. "The happy faces of those Episcopalians is what convinced me," said one man. "I knew it had to be real!"

Within a short time, many more members of the congregation received the Holy Spirit. Just as at Van Nuys, these were established members of the church who had been struggling to keep the church open. One woman had been at St. Luke's for over thirty years; most of the rest had belonged for ten, fifteen, or twenty years. The average age of these newly baptized Christians was probably fortyish, although one lady in her seventies was among the first to receive the Holy Spirit.

One of the stalwart old-timers was Monty, a man with a rich background in business and professional life. He was my bishop's warden (the minister's "right hand man" in the Episcopal polity) the first year at St. Luke's, and also the treasurer —which office he had held for ten years past. He had seen the little church go through its ups and downs, and finally settle into the downhill trend. Now all of a sudden he saw the trend sharply reversed, and he determined to find out why! For several weeks he sat in our meetings and observed us as objectively as he could—and he was a sociologist by profession!

"He makes me nervous!" commented one person. "He's just sitting there watching us, like a-a- watch-bird!" But one night after vestry meeting the "watch-bird" took me aside.

"My counselling technique is changing because of these Friday nights!" he said. He was at that time a probation officer working with troubled youngsters, in whom he took a deep interest. Now he found his compassion somehow deepening and his attitude subtly changing. The next week in the meeting, as we were all praying together, Monty gestured to me.

"Come here and give me a hand," he said. He was already beginning to speak in tongues!

After this I had a different kind of treasurer.

"Don't spend any extra money this month!" he would warn us, with a harried look, "we're way behind!" Then he would add with a grin:

"I'm not really worried—praise the Lord!"

And Monty was typical of the moving of God at St. Luke's. Very, very few of the people who were active members of the church were in any way distressed or offended by the new experience their friends were claiming. Those who did not see it as something for themselves said:

"Well, we aren't interested in this Holy Spirit Baptism, but we can see that the church is coming alive, and we're happy about it."

There was no division. Occasionally in the early days I would receive a complaint:

"These 'Holy Spirit' people are getting cliquish!"

All it would take would be a word:

"Break it up, people! Don't clump together at the coffee hour and talk about your experiences—get out among the flock and spread the word!" And they would do it. The little church had been torn by internal strife, but now it was obvious that the Love of God was actively at work—healing the wounds, bringing people together into real appreciation of one another.

As people began visiting St. Luke's from other denominations, we saw God's forethought in choosing a tolerably "high" Episcopal Church for a centre of witness, since the unfamiliar liturgical worship discouraged people from leaving their own churches and clustering together at St. Luke's. When members of other churches received the Holy Spirit we told them:

"Your own church is your mission field. You are welcome to come back here for fellowship and for teaching, but we want you to go and tell the good news to your own pastor and your own friends."

One of our people put it this way:

"St. Luke's is like a pilot light. We light the other burners!"

Again, as in Van Nuys, these people discovered the joy of praying together. They, too, began to meet on any possible occasion or with any excuse. The big difference was that there was no opposition, no wild rumours, no fear, and no secrecy. This church honoured the work of the Holy Spirit, and everyone knew it.

Another very clear sign of the fullness of the Holy Spirit in people's lives is their interest in the Holy Scriptures. I had been brought up to look at the Bible as a collection of religious literature—some of it wonderful, some not so wonderful, some valid, some invalid, but the whole thing a mixture from which the scholars could select and tell us what was authentic. To accept the Scriptures in their entirety as the work of the Holy Spirit was foreign to anything I had been taught, and yet that is exactly what I found myself being pressed to do as I continued in the life of the Spirit. It was not an intellectual decision; it was just that I could not be spiritually comfortable taking any patronizing or critical attitude toward that Book!

change in status
of Bible for them

Other Episcopalians began to experience the same thing. It wasn't so difficult for the layman who had been exposed to the arguments of "higher criticism," but for a minister, seminary trained, it was very hard. It's easy to get complicated, but it's awfully hard to return to simplicity! The people at St. Luke's simply began to rejoice in their newfound love for the Bible and to study it. I struggled with my intellect! One night at a study class a man from another parish expressed the usual "higher-critical" opinion of the Scripture. I tried to challenge him, but failed to be definite and convincing. I found myself spinning my wheels. Suddenly a woman in the class began to speak in tongues. I thought she was out of line in doing so, especially since she was a visitor from another church—a Presbyterian! No one had spoken aloud in tongues at the class before, and I didn't know how people would take it. This lady went on and on, and when at the end she began to repeat one phrase over and over, louder and louder, I decided it was time to do something! I looked at her, but her eyes were closed as she spoke—one hand lifted in praise. I started toward her, intending gently to ask her to stop, when she stopped of her own accord, and without a moment's pause, a man in the back of the class began to interpret. It was Toby. Toby was a big Norseman with a big voice; moreover he was a respected member of our Christian family, who had several times been impressively used to interpret when someone had spoken in tongues at a meeting.

"This is My Book! This is My Book! You read My Book! Don't criticise My Book! Just read My Book! For I am the Lord! I am the Lord! I am the Lord!" Toby's voice, like that of the speaker in tongues, got louder and louder until at the end he was nearly shouting. "I am the Lord! I am the Lord!"

What could one say? That class left greatly chastened and I never forgot the simplest way to define the Bible:

"This is My Book! I am the Lord!"

As I saw the people reading the Bible with great delight and seizing every opportunity to find out more about it, I thought of the years I had spent trying unsuccessfully to get people to read that Book, and I realized again how important is the Baptism in the Holy Spirit.

Although our membership did not increase with great rapidity, our church attendance did, because people who had been casual members, coming to church occasionally, when they felt like it, now were in church every Sunday, often two, three, and four times! What caused the change? Why did they come to church more than once on a Sunday and also pray together two or three times during the week? Not from a sense of duty, nor to show off devotion, but simply because they could not get enough of the fellowship of the Holy Spirit, which is a most tangible thing! For example, one Sunday morning at St. Luke's I turned from the altar to pronounce the ritual absolution to the people. As I did so, something I can only describe as a "wave of fellowship" hit me, coming up from the congregation, where over a hundred Christians were enjoying the Lord. I felt I had to shout "Hallelujah!" or do something to express the tremendous joy and love that engulfed me! I controlled myself, and continued with the liturgy, but I thought I was going to faint on the spot from sheer delight! The thing that led the early Christians to meet together even at the very risk of their lives was the tremendous joy of fellowship with Jesus and with one another through the Holy Spirit.

The profound test of spiritual experience, as the Bible points out quite often, is how people treat one another. The Apostle John said: "If any one says 'I love God,' and hates his brother, he is a liar . . ."[1] And the Apostle James says that there isn't much point in telling the beggar man who comes to you for help: "Go in peace, be warmed and filled!"[2] if you don't do anything to warm his body, and fill his stomach! The people at St. Luke's began to love one another and they began to be concerned about helping people. The first thing they wanted to do was to tell people about Jesus, but the Holy Spirit showed them that along with this they had to help in other ways.

A young man showed up in Seattle shortly after the initial receiving of the Holy Spirit at St. Luke's. Bill had a real concern for the "skid road" derelicts, especially the young ones. Quite on his own he started a sort of halfway house for men. Bill's idea was to deal with these men beyond the usual "skid-road" mission—helpful though it is. He wanted to bring his men away from the "road" into normal society where they could begin to regain their self-respect, and where they could receive real counsel and help.

St. Lukans began to have a new experience in that distasteful and unsavoury characters began to show up in the pews on Sunday morning or evening and in the prayer meetings. Many of these were just out of jail on a variety of charges: theft, alcoholism, drug-pushing, perversion, male prostitution, etc. They were received with real love. Our people took these men into their homes and sometimes would sit up nearly all night counselling with them. Many were led to Jesus, and real changes were made in their lives.

Members of minority groups began to visit and fellowship at St. Luke's, and they too were greeted, not with patronizing kindness, but with real brotherly and sisterly love; lines of colour and nationality melted away as thoroughly as had the walls of denominationalism.

The words of encouragement from the Lord at the beginning of my work at St. Luke's began to come true. At no time did we receive opposition from those in authority, either in the diocese or in the parish. The bishop was as good as his word and gave every kind of support he could. God had planted a tree of blessing at St. Mark's, Van Nuys, but it had been uprooted while just barely sprouting. Now it was transplanted at St. Luke's, Seattle, where in a climate of acceptance and understanding it began to flourish.

12
Every Need Supplied

Life in the Holy Spirit is different! Paul of Tarsus put it simply to his friends at Philippi: "My God will fill up all your needs in proportion to His riches in glory in Christ Jesus." [1] When we decided to go to Seattle, it was evident that we were going to be in a financial "bind." I was making a fairly decent income, for a minister, yet we had not saved any money, or even replaced our "early rummage sale" style furniture! Three teenagers make a dent in the budget! We didn't live extravagantly in any sense of the word, and yet every penny found its destination. I looked at Elberta.

"We're going to take a $4,000 cut in salary," I said. "Wonder what we're going to live on?"

"We've lived on a lot less," my wife replied. "Remember when you were in school we had a net income of $1,100 a year?"

"Uh-huh," I grunted, "I remember. We lived on that, and what the neighbours brought in! We used up, made do, wore out. I don't want to go back to *that*!"

"Well," said Elberta, "there's $3,000 in stock we inherited from Mum. We could always dip into that." Neither one of us had at this time quite realized what a good financial provider God is for His children.

When we left Van Nuys, we didn't bring our living-room furniture with us to Seattle—we took it to the dump! However, when we arrived in the Northwest we went straight to Sears and exercised our faith by picking out a new living-room ensemble and a carpet. Not only that, but it soon became evident, with three teenagers in the family, that we would have to have a second car, and so a little orange 1956 VW joined the family at the end of the year! Yet in spite of these expenses, and the reduction in income, we did not touch our little nest egg. God took care of us—in detail. It wasn't long before Elberta said:

"Let's not use that $3,000 on ourselves; let's save it for the kids—their education, or whatever."

I agreed, and our decision was immediately challenged. It was time to purchase new licence plates for our cars. The first car was already taken care of, but I needed $25 more to equip the "bug." What to do? I was just plain "out of money" until payday, still a week distant, and we needed that car. I took the matter to the Lord.

"Lord," I said, "I need $25 to licence that VW. As a matter of fact, I'm out of spending money and I could use $50!"

The next morning when I opened the mail there was a check for $43.72—an insurance dividend I wasn't expecting! But $43.72—why that amount? It seemed the Lord was saying to me:

"Dennis, if you want $25, ask for $25; if you want $50, ask for $50; but if you say '$25, or maybe $50,' I'll just split the difference!"

I remember another occasion that demonstrated His definiteness, and also the wonderful sense of humour—that's all you can call it—that our Lord displays with His children. I had purchased a typewriter, which was much needed at the church, but knowing that we were still limited in the budget, and yet wanting a good machine, I decided to pay for it out of my ministerial "discretionary fund." * This fund did not amount to very much, and it wasn't long before the first payment on the typewriter came due, and I didn't have the money! What now? Take the machine back? Maybe I had got ahead of the Lord in buying it. That night at the prayer meeting I found an envelope addressed to "Father Bennett" sitting on the piano. I opened it, and there was an anonymous gift of $50! I said:

"Thank you, Lord, but—the payment is $60 you know!" As the prayer meeting was breaking up, a young lady who was doing some volunteer stenographic work for me came up.

"Father Bennett," she said, "I haven't forgotten about that money you lent me from your discretionary fund, and I'll have it for you in the morning." Praise the Lord! I had forgotten that this young lady had borrowed $10 from my fund. This made up the $60!

"Thank you, Lord!" I said again. "That does it." But, alas, when I arrived home and looked at the bill, it was for $70! "Lord," I remonstrated, "I thought the monthly payment was for $60 and so that's what I asked for, but *You* knew it was for $70 all the time!"

But the next morning, Shirley handed me $20, not $10! I looked at her with surprise:

"That's right," she said. "Don't you remember I borrowed another $10 from you last month? I hadn't paid it back! I owe you $20." God does provide, and on time too!

It was the same with church finances. When I became vicar of St. Luke's, this little mission church was about $3,500 "in the red" in their operating budget, to say nothing of many

* A fund provided for the minister for miscellaneous expenses, especially charitable gifts—not for his personal use.

mortgages and loans they were attempting to pay off. It was a great pleasure to see God meet the financial needs, and as usual, He used interesting ways to do it! The income of the church was rising rapidly, because the Holy Spirit was urging people to tithe, but still some extra boosts were needed. After our fellowship and prayer meeting one night, one of my vestrymen found two one-dollar bills lying in the offering plate. He picked them up, and to his considerable surprise found a $100 bill lying beneath them. Upon retrieving the $100, to his astonishment he found nine more $100 bills with it! Someone—and we never found out who it was—had dropped $1,000 cash in that offering plate!

It was evident that we were going to be obliged to build a new meeting hall. Three hundred and more people were beginning to crowd into the little parish hall under the old church on Friday nights, so great was the interest in hearing about the blessing of Pentecost. But how could we build without capital?

"Lord," I said, "I'm just *not* going to have a capital funds drive. If you want us to have that new building, you'll have to send us the money!" I didn't even formulate in my mind what we would need to finance such a project. In the bank we had about $15,000 that had been given several years before in a building drive that had almost totally failed. (They were trying to raise $90,000.) Since it had been given for a new building it could not be used for any other purpose. I was sitting at my desk one afternoon, when in walked one of the faithful who had been at St. Luke's many years and had recently received the Holy Spirit. She put an envelope on my desk, saying:

"The Lord told me to give you this for the church." She turned quickly and walked away and was almost out of the building by the time I had opened the envelope. In it was a cheque for $10,000! I caught up with her at the street door.

the money comes!

"You can't do this!" I expostulated. "I know you don't have this kind of money!"

"I said the *Lord* told me to," she replied. "I sold some property, and He told me to give you that!" Nothing I could say would shake her resolve. $10,000 plus $15,000 made up the necessary capital to begin the new building! And so it went. As our budgeted income increased year by year, I watched the Lord meet every need.

One day I came into the office to find my treasurer looking a bit glum.

"What's the problem?" I asked him.

"The R's," Monty said sadly. "They're moving away, and taking over $1,000 a year pledge with them! *That'll* leave a hole!"

Next morning, in walked another good layman who had just completed a deal in real estate. Smiling broadly, he said, "Here's my tithe!" and he laid a cheque for $1,000 on the desk! He knew nothing about the other family moving away, but God knew—and filled the hole immediately!

We know that when money was needed on one occasion, to pay the temple tax, Jesus produced it miraculously through the coin found in a fish's mouth. Most people remember the time that the Lord found Himself faced with five thousand hungry people out in the desert.

"It'd cost a lot of money to feed this crowd," said Philip, one of His disciples. "What can we do?" In this case Jesus did not supernaturally produce the money to buy the food, but asked:

"What do you have on hand?"

Andrew answered, "There's a youngster here with some bread and fish he's brought with him for lunch, but what is the good of that for a crowd like this?"

And then Jesus proceeded to feed the five thousand from

the little fellow's lunch-box! I believe that happened because the Bible says it did, but I also believe it because Jesus did <u>something similar in my own house</u>! It was the day our daughter was married. Husbands can be thoughtless people, and I'm no different from the average. That day I brought sixteen people home to lunch without even warning my wife! She told me later what had happened.

"I stood in the kitchen and said, 'Lord, Dennis has brought these folks home with him, and You know I don't have food for this many. This casserole is large enough to feed only five or six, and I haven't time to go to the store. I don't want to say anything about this, so I'm going to put the food on the table and trust You to do the rest!" She did just that, and said to me later:

"You know, I just watched that food go round and round. They kept digging in, and digging in, and everyone seemed to get enough to satisfy him and there was enough left over to feed two more who arrived later in the afternoon!"

"My God shall fill up all your needs!"

I hadn't been at St. Luke's more than a week or two when another kind of need was presented.

"What's the matter, Al?" someone asked at the vestry meeting. "You look worried."

"It's my daughter-in-law," Al said. "She's in the Swedish Hospital waiting for surgery. Ulcerative colitis."

I learned that this young wife was hemorrhaging so badly and was in such critical condition that her doctor was urging immediate surgery to remove her colon—not a good operation for anyone, but especially not for an attractive young woman in her early twenties. I called on Karen in the hospital, and after a little time of getting acquainted, I said:

"Ever think about praying to be healed?"

healing

Her answer was diffident—obviously she hadn't.

"Do you mind if I pray for you?" No, she didn't, so I prayed. I called again later in the week. She seemed not unpleased to see me. Yes, the hemorrhaging was still going on, and, yes, the doctor was still fingering his scalpel impatiently!

"D'you mind if I pray again?" I queried. This time it seemed to me that her response was a little more interested, and again I prayed for her.

On my third visit she said:

"I still have the hemorrhage, and my doctor says I've got to have the surgery." But this time *she* asked *me*, "Would you pray for me again?" We prayed—and the hemorrhage stopped! For five months, week by week, we prayed for Karen —one jump ahead of the good doctor all the time.

"I'm scheduled for surgery next week," she would say.

"Does the doctor say you are in immediate danger so that you *must* have the surgery next week?" I would ask.

"No."

"Can you ask him to give you another week of grace?"

She did, he would consent, and we would pray some more. The doctor became a little more hopeful each time, and a little less eager to do the operation. Then came the victorious day when he said:

"Karen, I didn't expect it, but this thing has gone into complete remission. We'll postpone the surgery indefinitely!"

It must have been several months later that I met Rupe, a big, friendly man whom it would have been hard not to like. He was a teacher of reading skills and was establishing a reading institute nearby in the university district. We met Rupe through a mutual friend and parishioner, a commercial artist, who did much beautiful work for the church's printing department. She had solicited the resources of our print shop to help produce a brochure to publicize Rupe's new venture, thereby saving him quite a little money.

We all had dinner together at our house one evening, and Rupe, after we were well acquainted, shared with us his physical problem. Some time ago he had been hospitalized with severe pain which the doctor diagnosed as kidney stones. Whether this was correct or not, the pain masked the fact that Rupe had a seriously infected appendix, and while he was being treated for the kidney problem, the appendix ruptured. Before the condition was caught, peritonitis was raging through his abdomen. The infection had virtually destroyed his diaphragm, the big muscular wall that separates the abdominal cavity from the chest cavity and serves as the main breathing muscle. One lung was partly collapsed and Rupe's heart was displaced so far that it was on the wrong side of his chest.

"My diaphragm is like a limp rag, the doctors tell me," Rupe said. "It's not only paralysed, but it's full of holes! In fact," he went on, "they are intrigued that I am able to breathe at all. It seems I have learned to use my rib muscles for breathing, but they tell me I'll be in a respirator soon, and probably won't live too long. Right now my voice is weakened by this of course, and it is too high in pitch, which is a serious handicap in my profession."

"Do you believe in Jesus?" I asked.

"No," he replied frankly, "I can find no contemporary records of His ever having existed." Rupe was the son of a minister, but had lost his faith.

"Would you come to our prayer meeting tonight?" I pursued.

Rupe said later: "I had to say 'yes'; you'd just saved me about two hundred dollars!"

Rupe sat and listened that night at the meeting while one person after another stood up and testified to God's healing power. It seemed as though there were more healing testimonies than usual.

"I burned my finger badly last night while I was cooking the dinner," one woman said, "but my husband prayed for it, and look, it isn't even red!"

"I smashed my thumb working in my shop. It was all black and blue, but I prayed for it myself, and when I got up this morning there wasn't a sign of a bruise! Look! My doctor says it's impossible; isn't that great?"

Another person told of laying aside her glasses. "I had to take my glasses off," she said, "because as God began to heal my eyes, soon I couldn't see with my glasses *on*!"

Even more impressive was the story brought by one of our young people. It had happened the summer before while she was at the church youth camp. She slipped on the rocks while hiking up the creek bed the first day at camp, and cracked her ankle. The foot swelled up and became a beautiful black-and-blue.

"They took me to the doctor in Everett," Chris said. "He X-rayed it, and said: "Yes, it's broken all right!" The orders were to stay on crutches and put no weight on it at all. As soon as the swelling had gone down, the doctor said he would put a cast on it. It didn't sound like much fun to be spending the week at camp on crutches, so I said to two of my girl friends: 'At home the folks would pray for this ankle to be healed.' So we all went into the chapel, and Rochelle and the other girl laid their hands on my foot, and we asked *Jesus* to heal it. It stopped hurting right away! I didn't need the crutches anymore, so I put them down and went out and joined a baseball game! By that night all the swelling had gone, and by the next morning the black-and-blue colour was all gone too! The camp nurse and the clergy were pretty unhappy with me because I wouldn't use my crutches. In fact, they wrote a letter to my mother saying that they couldn't be responsible, and the insurance wouldn't cover my injury because I was refusing to co-operate in the treatment!"

I saw Rupe get up and leave a little before the meeting was over. I slipped out and caught up to him just as he got into his little Ford Anglia. I climbed into the seat beside him. He was obviously moved.

"I don't believe the things those people were saying in there are possible! I don't believe in that sort of thing!" he protested.

Then turning to me he said:

"But why did I weep while they were saying them?" He paused, then, almost fiercely, he blurted:

"Can you heal my diaphragm?"

"No, *I* can't," I responded, "but *God* can!" And so I put my hand on his shoulder and prayed.

"Dear Lord," I said, "we sure could use a miracle right about now!" Nothing visible happened and as Rupe drove away, I thought:

"Well, that will probably confirm him in his unbelief. Too bad."

A week went by. I had almost forgotten about Rupe, but was brought sharply and uncomfortably aware of him when I saw him again as he walked into our prayer meeting on Tuesday night, a big broad smile on his face!

Perhaps he's come to laugh at us, I thought to myself, but I was very wrong. As soon as the time came to share, Rupe was on his feet. He told about the prayer we had said in the car the week before and then he went on:

"Nothing seemed to happen that night, but yesterday my son and I were crossing the sound on the ferry when suddenly a terrific pain hit me in the diaphragm. I felt it tighten up, and I've been breathing normally ever since!"

Rupe went back to the doctor, whose curiosity was completely aroused by this man who was breathing normally without a diaphragm! So interested were the doctors that they scheduled an X-ray moving picture to be made of Rupe's abdomen.

"Your diaphragm is still full of holes—it's still a mess," said one of the doctors, "but it's *working*!"

That first wonderful experience with the power of God threw Rupe into a rather amazing state of mind! He still could not accept Jesus intellectually, yet he clearly saw God's power. He began to have other prayers answered, and it wasn't long before his intellect had to capitulate to his spirit. He received Jesus and was baptized in the Holy Spirit.

It would have been miracle enough if the story had ended there, but it didn't! Nearly two years later, Rupe was praying at home with two friends, after attending a prayer meeting at St. Luke's.

"We'd had a wonderful evening," Rupe said. "One woman's eyes had been healed and several other miracles had happened. We came back to my apartment, and were kneeling around the big hassock in my living room—Bill, Ellee his wife, and me. Suddenly Bill said: 'My hands are on fire! They're hurting me!' I said: 'Put 'em on me!' I shuffled around the hassock on my knees to where Bill and his wife were kneeling, and he laid his hands on my chest. I felt as though all my insides had fallen out! I sprang to my feet, and literally had to grab at my trousers to keep them from falling off; they were suddenly too loose. I had to struggle to get my coat unbuttoned, it was now so tight. The whole outward configuration of my body was changing as my internal organs were renewed and went back into their proper positions. My heart was thumping like a hammer, of course, and I felt it move three or four inches, back into its normal place under my breast-bone. Not only was my diaphragm restored, but my physical body was changed so much that I had to get all new suits!"

But there are needs for more than money, food, or healing. We hadn't been at our new church very long before my wife and I began to discover how important it was that we get away once in a while to rest and relax. One Monday morning— and Monday was the day we hopefully called our "day off" —we looked unhappily at the cloudy skies.

"Well, we didn't pick a very good day for a picnic, dear," I said to Elberta. "Looks like it's going to be pouring after a while. What'll we do?"

"Pray?"

! ! ! ! There it was again! Pray about the weather? Wasn't that carrying things a bit *too* far? Still—Jesus prayed about the weather, and He got results! He said, "The works that I do shall you do also, and greater things than these shall you do . . ." [2]

"Okay." So we prayed; but the clouds did not roll away, and the sun did not blaze forth!

"What do we do now?" I asked my wife.

"Let's start out," she replied, so we put the picnic basket into the car and headed for the mountains, I, personally, feeling very silly. If the weather was bad in Seattle, one thing was sure; it was worse up in the hills. As we rolled along, we talked about it.

"We prayed for good weather—I think we're supposed to keep on driving until we get to the good weather," said my wife. And that's just what we did. We had clouds all the way up into the mountains until we began to approach the area where we had wanted to picnic, and, lo and behold, the sun began to break through!

"Keep driving!" said my woman of faith, and in a few

miles we emerged into full sunshine, right at a beautiful little picnic spot where we had a lovely warm day by the river. When we had eaten and basked in the sunshine for a while, we packed our things and headed back for town. We hadn't driven twenty minutes before we were in rain! Coincidence? Well, as a certain bishop of our acquaintance puts it: "All I know is that when I stop praying, the coincidences stop happening!"

Our next experience with "weather prayers" took place the following year. I had been invited to speak at several places in the San Francisco area. We had decided to drive to San Francisco and make our return journey up the Oregon coast as neither of us had ever seen the famous and beautiful Oregon coastline. The day before we were to make this journey, I flew to Eugene, Oregon, to make an address, and had ample opportunity to observe that all of Northern California and Oregon was under a solid deck of clouds. The weather on the ground in Oregon was rainy, and the airplane was almost refused permission to land because of marginal visibilities. I said to my wife:

"We aren't going to see the Oregon coast in very good weather. I've seen what it looks like from above!" Nevertheless, the next day we set out. When we got about one hundred miles north of San Francisco, sure enough, we started to go under the solid bank of clouds that I had flown over the day before. It hadn't changed much! We stopped that night at a little motel along the way, and in the morning, looking at the still threatening skies, I said to Elberta:

"Let's pray for sunshine on the Oregon coast!"

And so we did. We agreed for good weather on the Oregon coast, and then continued to drive through Northern California under increasingly gloomy clouds.

When it is raining in Northern California, you do not expect it to be sunshiny in Oregon, and besides that, we who live in the Northwest know that the weather normally becomes worse, not better, as we go out toward the coast! Everything was working against our prayer, and yet as we approached the Oregon border, the skies suddenly began to lighten! Exactly as we crossed the border, the sun came out. By the time we had driven a mile into Oregon, the last of the scattered clouds had disappeared and we were driving in beautiful warm sunshine! All the way from there to Tillamook we saw the Oregon coast in the most beautifully clear weather imaginable. We stopped several times along the way during the day, and people would say:

"It's funny; this set out to be such a gloomy day, and then all of a sudden it changed!"

Arriving at Tillamook, we turned inland, and in twenty minutes we were driving in the pouring rain! God had answered our prayer with His accustomed exactness—we had asked for "sunshine on the Oregon coast," and that is exactly what He provided!

People ask, when you talk about "weather prayers":

"But what if you are praying for sunshine, and someone else is praying for rain?" The answer is simple: It'll rain on him, and the sun will shine on you!

It was while on the trip that culminated in the "sunshine-on-the-Oregon-coast" experience that I had underlined for me another aspect of "my God shall supply all your need." One of my assignments had been to spend a week on the Stanford University campus, and to preach at the Stanford Chapel on Sunday morning. I remembered my preaching classes in theological school.

"Now," our professor would say, "you gentlemen must remember that you should put in at least thirty hours of preparation each week on your sermon!" This was the way the "great preachers" did it, we were given to understand, and who didn't want to be a "great preacher"? Alas, we overlooked the fact that the "great preachers" had "great secretaries" to keep files of information, and to read, type, correct, etc., and that most of *us* would be going out to undermanned, underpaid, under-equipped situations, where we would be working twelve hours a day just to keep up with the administrative and pastoral needs of the people, and probably cranking a mimeograph and licking stamps, too; to say nothing of sweeping floors and stoking furnaces! It didn't take us long to realize that three hours a week for the sermon would be hard enough to find, let alone thirty!

I enjoyed preaching and seemed to do it pretty well, but I never went into the pulpit without a prepared manuscript. I didn't always follow it exactly, but it was there. After receiving the Holy Spirit, however, I found that I was unable to feed the people on Sunday with food I had prepared the previous Wednesday! Instead I found myself laying my manuscript aside and beginning to speak the words which the Spirit gave me on the spot. Before, when I had tried to preach extemporaneously I had simply rambled, but now after the service people would say:

"How did you know that I needed to hear *that* this morning? You answered the exact question that has been troubling me!"

I discovered that a sermon does not have to be a literary masterpiece, but it should be more like "scratch feed," with something for everyone! From then on, and since coming to St. Luke's in Seattle, I had been preaching without a manuscript, my only preparation being that I had been working with people during the week, praying, and reading the Scripture. The raw material was there, and I trusted the Holy Spirit to put it together. Indeed, it was fortunate for me that I could work this way, for sometimes I was called upon to speak or

Shed his
manuscript

preach anywhere from six to ten times in a week, and it would have been impossible to prepare all those addresses beforehand, and deadly to the work of the Holy Spirit to deliver a "canned" speech, even one I had prepared myself. But here was an invitation to preach at the Stanford Chapel—the "Harvard of the West". The Tempter was quick to point out to me:

"Think of the students and faculty in the congregation. You'd better write out *this* sermon for sure! This is no time for the 'off-the-cuff' sort of thing!"

I had the grace to reply: "If the Holy Spirit can give me the words for the people of Seattle, He can give them for the people here. Get lost, Satan! In Jesus' Name!"

And when I stood up to speak on that Sunday morning, sure enough the words were there; and that week, in that great academic centre, a number of young men and women were filled with the power of God.

13
God's-Incidents

"Anne?" The voice on the telephone was trembling with anxiety.

"Yes? What's the matter, Peggy?"

"Oh, Anne, I'm so worried. Chuck left on a sales trip yesterday and gave me a $300 cheque to deposit in the bank. He's going to be depending on it, and I've mislaid it. I can't find it anywhere!" Peggy was on the verge of tears. "Will you call some of the others and ask them to pray, too, please!"

"Of course I will!" Anne hung up on the phone and went to work on it. Anne and Peggy and "the others", members of a nearby Episcopal church, had received the Baptism in the Holy Spirit at St. Luke's in that first year. Typically, they did not leave their own church, but were trying in every way to get their own parish to see the importance of what had happened to them.

Peggy began cleaning up the breakfast dishes, but her mind was still very much on the missing cheque when after a bare half-hour, the phone rang. It was Anne.

"Peg, the cheque is in the laundry, under a pile of clothes."
Peggy looked hastily and, sure enough, there it was!

check incident

Clairvoyance? No! God forbids that sort of thing. Anne was not exercising some kind of ability in "extrasensory perception"; instead, God simply gave her a Gift of Knowledge and showed her where the cheque was as she prayed.

Shift the scene to winter of that same year. It's snowing—hard. The vicar of St. Luke's has just been asked to make a call at King County Hospital, Unit II, on Queen Anne Hill. Queen Anne Hill is one of the more confusing parts of Seattle and I was not even aware that there was a hospital of any kind in that vicinity! Nevertheless, I climbed into the car and took off. I was perhaps halfway to my destination when suddenly I realized that in all my rush I had forgotten to look up the address and to figure out the location of the hospital! Bother! Now I would have to stop along the way to get information. It was snowing harder than ever, and there were several inches of wet slush on the sidewalks. Suddenly, I thought:

Look here, I'm a Christian, filled with the Holy Spirit. The Holy Spirit knows where that hospital is, and if He can guide me to speak in a language I've never learned, He can guide this car as I drive it! So I went on, determining to drive the car as I felt led, trusting the Lord. I had no special feelings about it, and saw no guardian angel leading me down the road! I just simply drove on, and coming to Mercer Avenue, I was inclined to turn left, which I did. Then left again on to Queen Anne and up the steep hill. When I got to Boston Avenue, a street I did not even know existed, I was again inclined to turn, this time to the right. After driving a few more blocks, there, to my admitted amazement, I saw the hospital for which I was looking!

On another occasion it was Christmas Eve, and I had to make a last-minute shopping foray into the heart of one of Seattle's busiest areas. Before I arrived at my destination I prayed, and had assurance that there would be a parking place awaiting me! Sure enough, there it was as I pulled up in front of the store—right by the crosswalk a car was pulling out, leaving time on the meter! Coincidence? Well, about two weeks later, again at the very busiest time of day, I had to go to the same store. Again I prayed, and the very same parking place was waiting for me! After this sort of thing happens repeatedly, one ceases to say "coincidence", but says instead "God's-incidents"!

One of our church members lived for a time on Bainbridge Island and had to cross on the ferry daily to come to work. His was a later ferry than most, and when he arrived at the terminal each morning the parking lots were already jammed, except for one parking place, right by the entrance to the boarding ramp. That one was always waiting for him!

"What about speaking in tongues? Surely this, too, played a part in the experience of the early years at St. Luke's?" Yes, it certainly did!

One St. Lukan felt led to go once a week to the County Hospital to visit the wards where there were lonely and aged folk who didn't have anyone to care. Here she was like an angel of mercy, and many were helped and brought to Jesus by her "unofficial" ministrations. One day she stopped to to speak with a little man who was sitting on the side of his bed looking sad.

"May I pray with you?" she asked.

He looked at her even more sadly, and replied:

"I no spik! I no spik!" But this did not frustrate the Holy Spirit, or her. She felt that God wanted her to talk to this little man, and if he did not understand her language she would have to trust God to give her words to say, so she opened her mouth and began to speak just as "the Spirit gave utterance." She did not understand the words she said, but to her delight the little man opened his eyes wide in amazement as he leaned over and with trembling hands drew a little book, obviously a New Testament, out of his bedside table drawer.

"Canary Island Spanish!! Canary Island Spanish!!" he said, tapping the little book with his forefinger, while his eyes shone with excitement and joy. His visitor bowed her head and began to pray for him, still accepting the words that the Spirit gave her, and the little man spoke every syllable right with her. She was speaking his language, and although she did not understand a word she was saying, she knew from his actions that she was reaching his heart with comfort from the Lord!

The husband of another of the "faithful women" received the Baptism in the Holy Spirit. He had been a consistent scoffer for many years, but when his wife received the Holy Spirit and he began to see miracles happening in his own family, he became interested and asked for and received this experience himself. His "tongue" was strikingly oriental, so much so that one day, while on his delivery route—he drove a delivery van—he encountered a Chinese customer, and boldy spoke some words in his "tongue"! The Chinese man answered him in the same dialect. Bob spoke again, and the Chinese person again responded, then asked in English:

"Where did you learn to speak my language?"

"What language is it?" Bob inquired.

"Why it's Mandarin, of course," the other replied, "and you speak it perfectly!"

"What did I say?"

"You greeted me, and I returned your greeting. Then I suggested that since you spoke my language, you should take a trip to the Orient with me next year and meet my family. You replied:

" 'I can't go now, but I will go later.' "

Sometime later, this man was at a prayer meeting and in the course of the evening spoke in his new tongue. There was an interpretation in English expressing praise to God. Present at the meeting was a Chinese woman, the wife of a medical doctor, and an exchange student at the University of Washington. She spoke up:

"How can this man speak Mandarin so perfectly? Where did he learn such beautiful Mandarin?"

Where indeed—?

One day, at about ten o'clock in the morning, my wife Elberta felt a strong impression:

"Pray for Steve!"

Steve, our older son, was in his senior year in high school. His mother was given no indication of why she should pray, or what for—just "Pray!" She prayed as the Holy Spirit gave her the words. How else could she pray? The New Testament says: "We know not what to pray for as we ought, but the Spirit Himself makes intercession for us, with unsayable utterances." [1] Elberta let the Spirit make intercession for Steve by giving her the words. After praying for a few minutes in a language unknown to her, she felt that the job was done, so she stopped. At four o'clock that afternoon Steve walked into the house.

"You prayed for me at 10 o'clock this morning, Mum!" he said. She never found out what it was that she was praying for —he didn't tell her, but he had known and felt the power of her prayer when he needed it.

A similar, although more dramatic example of the same thing took place near this time. A Presbyterian family—father, mother, and two sons—had received the Holy Spirit, and become part of an interdenominational prayer group meeting in the neighbourhood. Another member of the group, a Lutheran, was a jet captain for a major airline. One night, Earl, the captain, was on a trip overseas. Betty, the mother of the first-

*the aeroplane &
prayer*

mentioned family, was awakened with a strong urge from the Holy Spirit:

"Pray for Earl!" No data, just the urge to pray. Again, what choice did she have? She prayed as the "Spirit gave the utterance," in an unknown tongue, until the burden of prayer was lifted. She fell back to sleep, and did not think too much more about it until Earl returned to the neighbourhood meeting from his flight.

"We had a rather hair-raising experience at our destination this trip," he said. "We were holding in solid instrument weather, awaiting landing clearance from the tower. When the permission came, due to an error, two airliners were cleared on the same approach, and as we broke out of the clouds we were frighteningly close together, and for a few moments it looked as though we were going to collide. My co-pilot was at the controls. To my surprise he made no effort to manoeuvre us away from the other ship, but just held his course and allowed the other aircraft to get out of our way. After we had successfully and safely rolled out, and turned off on to the taxi-way, my co-pilot said:

"Captain, that was a very strange thing. You know, when I saw the spot we were in, I naturally felt that I should make some effort to get out of there, but my hands and feet were just frozen to the controls. I couldn't move them at all! Now I realize that if I had tried to change the attitude of the airplane in some way, we might have been in serious trouble. The safest thing I could have done was just hold the course."

When Earl said this, Betty of course spoke up and told of her prayer during the night, and when times were compared they found that her prayer "in the Spirit" was offered exactly at the moment of the danger over that distant city!

"These signs shall follow them that believe . . ." said Jesus, and sure enough they do! But just as wonderful as these gifts of the Holy Spirit are the fruits of the Holy Spirit—the love, joy, and peace that begin to show in the lives of people who are truly beginning to trust Jesus.

One night, at about 10.30, my wife and I were just about ready to turn in when suddenly the front door burst open and in came our two sons, faces flushed with excitement.

"Mum, Dad! Do you know what just happened?" Steve flung himself into a chair, and Conrad followed suit.

"We were taking the girls home after the ball game, and we stopped at the drive-in in Ballard to get a hamburger and a coke. Con and I were waiting at the counter, when suddenly two fellows came up and just pushed their way in ahead of us. Well, we didn't like that very well, so we shoved back into our place."

"Yeah," broke in Conrad, the younger. "Then they yelled, and grabbed us from behind. I really thought we were going to have to let 'em have it!"

"What happened then?" I asked apprehensively. The boys didn't seem to be damaged in any way—I knew they were both very capable of taking care of themselves.

"It was the funniest thing," said Steve. "Both of us swung around. I know my fists were ready, and I'm pretty sure Conrad's were too." He looked at his brother, who nodded.

"I was going to 'deck' my guy, I know that. But as I swung around, my hands just sort of fell to my sides, and my fists came open, and I found myself saying:

'I can't hit you. I'm a Christian!' "

"And exactly the same thing happened to me," his brother said.

"Yeah. But even funnier, when I said that, those two tough characters literally turned pale, and ran for their lives!"

One Sunday morning after the 11 o'clock service, as I greeted a pleasant-looking young fellow and his petite wife, he said:

"We were kind of disappointed."

"What do you mean, sir?" I inquired, as I shook his hand.

"Well, my wife and I, we're Roman Catholics, you see, and we'd heard about this church. So we came to see what was going on. And—well, nobody *did* anything. I mean, it was a real nice service, but we thought somebody would, er, speak in tongues or—or something," he ended, a little lamely.

I laughed. "Oh, I see what you mean! Well, that doesn't usually happen on Sunday morning. There are people visiting who might not understand, you know. Why don't you come to our prayer meeting on Tuesday evening? It is very informal, and you are likely to hear the gift of tongues and interpretation."

"Oh, but it was wonderful just the same!" his wife broke in, her eyes positively sparkling with enthusiasm. "Why, those people certainly love God, don't they? I mean, you can feel it! I've never been to a mass where the people were so intent on the Lord!"

They went on down the steps and I turned to greet another stranger, who was somewhat shabbily dressed.

"I just want to tell you, Father Bennett," he said squeezing my hand earnestly, "that two of your men prayed with me for nearly three hours last Friday night, and they got me straightened out, too!" The man's voice shook just slightly as he added:

"I never dreamed anyone would care enough to take that much time with me and my problems."

" 'Lo, how these Christians love one another!' " Well—yes, more and more! And this is the greatest of all manifestations of the Holy Spirit! "The greatest of these is love." Not human love, but God's love in people: drawing them together, bringing them to forgive one another, and reaching out to others in need of love and forgiveness—this, as Paul said, is the greatest. But, as Paul also said, we need the other too—the miraculous manifestations of God's power. It isn't "gifts *or* fruits," but "gifts *and* fruits" of the Spirit that we need, and at St. Luke's we began to see them both.

14
The Valley of Baca

"The way I've got it figured, Dennis, it's all downhill from now on!" Bob grinned at me happily. He had received the Baptism with the Holy Spirit two days before, and like most of us at that point, felt that he "had it made"! I well remember the first week after my own receiving the Holy Spirit. Amazing! What were those old-time saints having such a struggle about, anyway? It was all very simple! When I arose in the morning—there was God! Who could help but praise Him? At night, I fell asleep listening to the Holy Spirit in my heart saying:

"Praise the Lord!"

All day long I felt His Presence with me. When I had to speak, He provided the words. When we prayed, things happened. What was all the problem? Yes, I knew what Bob meant. I don't remember exactly how long this "free ride" lasted for him, but for me it had been about one week!

What happened then? I lost my temper! Parents of teenage children will have sympathy when I explain that I got angry with one of our sons! He hadn't done anything so awful; in fact, I don't even remember the cause of my anger, but I was furious beyond all reason. I had considered myself a good-natured fellow, rather mild—certainly not bad-tempered in any sense of the word, except that now and then, you know, one had to give vent to one's irritation! Oh, there was the mark on the breakfast-nook wallpaper where I had hurled a tuna sandwich one lunchtime in a fit of frustration, and the hole in the masonite picnic table I had put my fist through while emphasizing a point with one of our children! It was a kind of family joke that now and then, as my kids phrased it, "Daddy blew his top!" Those same children could calculate pretty accurately just about how far I could be pushed without detonating! If they went too far, they took the consequences with philosophical aplomb!

But, you see, Satan had this weak spot all picked out. He had been nurturing it for years. I had a temper—I was sometimes impatient and irritable—and this was the means by which he tripped me up. As a result, when my son got into trouble one night, I lost my temper. I yelled, I swore, I stamped my foot; *in fine* I made a complete fool of myself, and when I was through with my tantrum, the devil whispered to me:

"Filled with the Holy Spirit, eh?"

My anger drained away as quickly as it had come. I was crushed. I apologized to my son, who had of course taken my pyrotechnics in his stride as a "to-be-expected" reaction. I went to bed that night a sad and discouraged person. All my joy was gone. There was no spontaneous praise in my heart as I addressed myself to sleep; instead, the words of the Bible came to me: "They crucify to themselves the Son of God afresh, and put Him to an open shame." [1] For the first time in my life, I *wept* for my sins.

When I awoke the next morning, my heart was still very heavy. I had lost the blessing—would I ever get it back? I thought back over the events of the past week, and I said:

"Praise the Lord anyway!" And as I did so, joy flooded back into me, and again tears came to my eyes as I realized how much God puts up with, and how ready He is to forgive.

It was the beginning of a long time of getting up and falling down. I was disappointed to find that I hadn't suddenly been made perfect! But I did begin to understand that the Holy Spirit, Who had come to live in me when I'd first accepted Jesus so many years before, was now, through my baptism in the Holy Spirit, at work in my soul in a tremendous new way. At salvation my *spirit* had been made perfect, but I was to find that even after my Pentecost, my soul or psychological nature was not perfect, and would take time and effort to be brought into line. The *soul* and not the spirit was where the "hangups" were: the bad temper, the emotional upsets and complexes, the wrong thinking, the mixed up reactions—and some of them were very firmly entrenched. Now in receiving the Holy Spirit,* I had opened my psychological being—mind, will, and emotions—to be inundated or "baptized" in Him, so that He could really clean up the mess in my soul—but it wouldn't happen overnight!

It was only a few weeks after Elberta and I had both received the Baptism in the Holy Spirit that we received warning of a coming time of trial that would be the most severe we had yet experienced. Our doctor had expressed concern about Elberta. He felt that he should operate and remove what he hoped and expected would be a benign growth. She had had a similar surgery several years before without problem, and for this reason was not over concerned, although she did consent to be prayed for at the altar before the operation. The

---

* Receiving the Holy Spirit, or being "baptized in the Holy Spirit," does not mean "getting the Holy Spirit," but "receiving" or "making welcome," permitting the Holy Spirit to fill more areas of our lives, and to flow out through us to the world.

doctor had explained to us that if the growth was malignant, they would proceed without delay to perform a radical mastectomy (removal of the breast), so that the patient would not know the extent of the surgery until she came out of the anesthetic.

I had tried to share Elberta's optimism, but it was an anxious time in the waiting room of the Valley Presbyterian Hospital the next morning. When, after three hours, the surgeon came out to talk with me, my heart sank as I saw his serious face. The biopsy showed malignant tissue, and they would have to continue into radical surgery. Later that day, while my wife was still in the recovery room, our doctor tried to explain to me what a shattering blow this would be to her, both physiologically and psychologically, and how long it would take her to adjust. I was, of course, terribly shaken by it all, and dreaded my first visit with Elberta after the surgery. How would I find the strength and conviction to give her the courage she needed?

Both the doctor and I had under-estimated Elberta—and the Lord! I found her smiling—"glowing" would be a better word, seemingly unperturbed at the catastrophe which had overtaken her. Elberta had a firm hold on her victory in the Spirit even though physically she was in deadly combat. She proceeded to leave the hospital in half the time the doctor had predicted. Within two weeks she was able to be in church. There were over five hundred people at the family Eucharist that morning, yet Elberta seemed to me to stand out like a gentle beacon.

But we weren't through the woods yet! The doctor prescribed a course of cobalt radiation for her, just to be sure. Some who had been through it said the effect of this treatment was worse than the surgery! Radiation sickness was inevitable—nausea, weakness, lowered blood count. And sure enough, as she started through the treatment, Elberta began to have all the expected reactions, plus one more—the radiation began to thicken her oesophagus, and she developed a distressing lump in her throat that troubled her a great deal.

Some weeks after Elberta's surgery, we had a guest speaker at our evening service, a well-known leader of the healing movement in the Episcopal Church. After the service she came to our home, and met with a number of people who were interested in the work of the Holy Spirit. In the course of the evening, without having time to say anything to our guest about the nature of the problem, we asked her to pray for Elberta. We all joined with her in prayer, of course.

From then on, the lump-in-the-throat symptoms disappeared, and not only that, my wife went through the entire series of cobalt radiation treatments with no further symptoms of radiation sickness at all. She confounded the doctors and nurses in attendance each time she walked into the treatment room, submitted to the therapy, and then simply walked out again as if nothing had happened, while other patients were temporarily exhausted and debilitated. Not only did she have no nausea or weakness, but her blood count went up instead of down ! She had suffered from serious anaemia all her life, but now she discontinued using an iron supplement she had needed for years. She began to enjoy a physical vigour she had never known—even her need for sleep was sharply reduced. The surgeon said that if there were no further trouble within five years, Elberta would be in the clear.

Then, shortly after our coming to Seattle in 1960, just about a year after the first surgery, the enemy struck again. The malignancy was recurring ! There were new tumours in the breast area. As far as the doctors were concerned this was a death sentence. There was nothing more to be done, except to try by various means to slow down the growth of the disease. In a basic attempt to do this, the surgeon urged an operation to remove the ovaries, and Elberta consented to it. Again came the doctor's warnings of the results of this procedure: there would be a premature menopause, with attendant symptoms, depression, and other side effects. None of these things took place! Elberta had no lasting symptoms from the surgery, and continued to enjoy her newfound vigour—but the tumours continued to grow.

At the time of the first surgery, in Van Nuys, Elberta had said to me:

"You know, Dennis, while I was under the anesthetic, the Lord said to me: 'Will you take all this out of Satan's hands and give it to me?' I said, 'Yes, Lord.' I know He has His hand on this whole situation. I'm not worried about it at all."

Now she said:

"I'm not going back to the doctor or the hospital. They have done all they can. I've put this thing in God's hands, and He has everything under control." Elberta did not take this stand because she was ungrateful to the doctors—she had accepted and had appreciated their ministrations, but now she had given the case to God completely, and there it was to stay.

The next two years were the happiest and most fruitful my wife had ever known. She once confessed to me:

"Before I received the Holy Spirit, at times I used to get so bored and depressed with the prospect of years and years of church bazaars, rummage sales, ladies' guilds, fashion shows, etc., that I felt I just couldn't go on!"

Now things were different for her. She still hardly ever opened her mouth in a meeting. Once she commented about her role in this way: "I just occupy a chair!" But quietly and effectively she counselled and helped many people, and earned their respect and love.

Our family all depended on her strength, and no one leaned on her more than I did. Elberta wasn't a highly trained theologian. She had never attended Bible school or seminary, but she read the Scriptures almost continuously since being baptized with the Holy Spirit, and she was equipped with that wonderful and blessed characteristic known as common sense. She felt that her place was at home, keeping an eye on our maturing family, although she did occasionally make a "missionary journey" with me. She disliked "making speeches," but when needful could give a good account of herself. Things like clothes and fashion were of little interest to her; yet she always looked neat and pretty.

The weeks went by, and the months. Still she enjoyed physical vitality, but the malignant sores in her body ate away, and gave no sign of abating. Every night I would anoint her and pray. Her friends were praying. The church was praying. Yet although we had intercessions as a part of the church service, so surely did she feel that the whole matter was in God's hands, that for a long time she did not want public prayer to be made for herself. Finally one night, I said:

"Honey, I just can't go to that altar and pray for everyone else, and not pray for you." So she consented.

Early in 1963, she began to have difficulty in breathing if she exerted herself beyond an ordinary pace. It was evident that the disease was working in her lungs. Her trust in God was unshaken. I commented to her one day on her faithfulness in praying and reading the Scriptures. She said:

"When you are facing the possibility of death daily, it makes a difference!" Death was one thing she did not fear at all.

She wanted to keep her mind on God all the time. If I would thoughtlessly sit down at the piano and play light opera or sing some popular song, she would say:

"That's the wrong tune!" This wasn't because she was being puritanical. She explained:

"I want to have the right kind of music running in my mind. If I listen to 'Oklahoma,' or 'South Pacific,' I'll wake up in the morning humming the words to 'I'm Going to Wash that Man,' or 'The Surrey with the Fringe on Top'! I want to have songs about God running in my mind, and wake up singing *them*!"

In June of that year I was asked to go to Alaska for several days to speak for Episcopalian and Full Gospel* groups in Anchorage and Fairbanks. I didn't want to leave Elberta. She was beginning to have real difficulty in breathing if she put forth more than minimal effort, but she insisted that I carry out the mission, and so, reluctantly, I went. She was in no pain, and was able to function quite normally in every way. No one would have known by talking ot her that there was anything physically wrong with her. When I returned from Alaska, she said:

"You know, Dennis, while you were away, my lungs began to fill with fluid. I knew that the doctor would drain that fluid if I asked, but I had determined not to turn to man for help. I went to the altar at the church and just said: 'Lord, you'll have to help me because my whole trust is in You,' and He immediately took care of it, and I was fine!"

By the middle of July, however, she was having to sit up in a chair to sleep at night, to help her breathing. Still, during the day she was able to lead a comparatively normal life. By the last of the month she was forced to remain seated on the couch in the front room day and night, and she began to have real pain. Still she was adamant. She would not have a doctor, nor would she go into hospital. She would not accept any painkiller or drug, not even so much as an aspirin tablet. Hers was not a sickroom, but a battleground.

---

* "Full Gospel" is one of the terms used for those Christian groups that teach not only salvation through Jesus Christ, and other essentials of the Christian Faith, but also the Baptism in the Holy Spirit.

Elberta's illness & death

The combat became fiercer. At night I slept on the floor in the front room. The one thing she wanted me to do was to play and sing gospel songs. They helped her to sleep at night; they helped her to get through the day. Good friends assisted me in nursing her. Two wonderful doctors were hovering in the background. One of them said to me:

"Dennis, she's choosing the right way. There's nothing we could do." But they were afraid for what might be yet to come. I knew what they feared.

She continued to get worse. For a week she ate nothing, beyond a few sips of bouillon; yet there was not any visible loss of weight or pallor. At this time one of our sons said:

"Dad, I've never seen Mum look so beautiful!"

The pain was very bad, and yet it was never more than she could handle. She fought it out with the enemy toe-to-toe—her mind clear, and unfogged by drugs. Being unable to persuade her to take any kind of medicine, I said:

"Honey, won't you accept at least a little oxygen to make your breathing easier?" She did so, for my benefit I think, because she must have known how helpless I felt. Throughout that day, off and on, she took some oxygen. Then after a while Elberta said softly:

"Take it away."

It was evident that she was growing weaker, but she was peaceful and seemed in a lot less pain. As evening drew on, while our three children and I were there with her, I said:

"I love you."

She said: "I love you."

I said: "Praise the Lord!"

She said: "Praise Him!" And very simply, with no struggle, she died.

One of our doctor friends said a short time later: "Her death is a miracle!" He was fearing hemorrhages and nausea, and all the horrors that can accompany a cancer death, but Satan's hand was limited.

<u>Elberta's death was surrounded by victory</u>. It was more like a soldier's death—a martyr's death. Half-an-hour after she died, my older son came to me and said:

"Dad, I saw Mum go into heaven!"

"What do you mean, Steve?" Stephen at twenty was a very practical young man, very much like his mother in an apparent lack of sentimentality; he was certainly not given to romanticizing.

"Why," he said, "about ten minutes after she died, the whole room faded away, and I found myself standing on the bank of a great river. A little boat was there, and I saw Mum get into the boat and go across the river. Jesus met her on the other side, and I saw them go up the grassy bank, laughing and talking together. I could see the beautiful city in the background; and before she left, she turned and waved at me! I know she saw me, too!"

At the same time, a mile across town, some friends had heard of Elberta's death and were weeping about it. Suddenly Claudia, one of the teenage girls in the family, started to laugh:

"Why," she said, "I see Elberta! She's going across a green field, laughing and talking with Jesus!"

The Lord did not cease to give signs of His blessings, even during the funeral and burial. When we went to select the coffin, I feared this would be a terrible ordeal. I looked at the various elaborately decked-out caskets, none of which seemed to be right. The mortician, a personal friend of mine, and characteristically helpful and understanding, was trying his best. Suddenly I turned and saw it! A bronze casket, simple and handsome; on each of the handle plates there was a portrayal of the Last Supper, and at each corner there was the figure of an angel! It was as if it suddenly dropped from heaven.

"This is the one!" I said. Though I'd officiated at hundreds of funeral services, I had never seen another like it.

The funeral was an affirmation of her victory in Christ. Bishop Lewis, who had stood with us so firmly in our coming to Seattle, celebrated the Lord's Supper, while the people of St. Luke's crowded into the little church with feelings of mingled joy and sorrow.

As we stood around her grave, we began to sing spontaneously, "Praise God from Whom all blessings flow!" We knew that although the mortal body was laid away with honour, Elberta was not there, but with Jesus in His Kingdom, where one day we too would rejoice with her when our course was run.

15
A Crown of Life

For some time after Elberta's death I seemed spiritually to be in a kind of limbo. There was no doubt that she had won through to victory, but it was a victory that left her on the other side of that great river Stephen had seen in the vision. She had gone on into the City of God, and she was with Jesus, but she had gone. She wasn't with me anymore, and I missed her very much.

There was much misunderstanding and bitterness in my soul. What could I now say about answers to prayer, especially prayer for healing? Had not God failed or refused to heal just when healing was most needed, when the one human being dearest to me had not been healed?

The Baptism in the Holy Spirit had opened my eyes, and I had come to see, all the way through the Bible, how God was ready to help His people even in their simplest physical needs. He was involved in every detail of their lives. I had come to see that God was the same for this present day, and to trust Him to heal a cold, a burned finger, or to guide in the seeming little things of life—like jobs, and parking places! This wasn't because one wanted to get things from God, as much as because one wanted to experience God's reality and closeness and love. Before receiving the Holy Spirit I had known God's leadings and answers to prayer in what seemed like a far too infrequent kind of way. Now I had had a taste of what it was like to live in a new relationship, in which God did, as the Scripture said, "supply all your need." [1] Was I going to have to return to that uncertain world where God sometimes did and sometimes didn't? A place where you couldn't really depend on Him? Where every prayer had to be ended with what has been called the "faith-destroying phrase": "If it be Thy will . . ."?

The evening of Elberta's death, after everyone had either gone home or gone to bed, I sat down and opened the Bible, looking at random for something that might speak to me. My eyes fell on these words in the Book of the Prophet Ezekiel:

"Also the word of the Lord came unto me, saying: Son of man, behold, I take away from thee the desire of thine eyes with a stroke . . . and at evening my wife died . . ." [2]

It was too pointed a reference to be a coincidence, but what did it mean?

Again the next evening I opened the Bible, and this time a verse in the Book of Isaiah presented itself to me at once:

"The righteous perisheth, and no man layeth it to heart . . . none considering that the righteous is taken away from the evil to come." [3]

Since Elberta had been gone I had taken to walking around the neighbourhood first thing in the morning. It seemed to help somehow. There were still some flowers blooming, and as I walked and admired the gardens which are so much a part of the crisp beauty of Seattle, I had a feeling that Elberta was walking in the gardens of God's Kingdom, enjoying their beauty. It wasn't that I sensed her presence with me. I knew that any kind of imagined contact with the departed was utterly forbidden by God and that Elberta was in no sense still in or even adjacent to this world; but it was as if there were a parallel experience and it gave me comfort. As I walked along on this particular autumn morning, I asked God:

"How come Elberta died?"

His response was immediate, in that "still, small voice," not an answer to my question, but a statement:

"She was one of my great ones!"

"I know that, Lord," I replied. He brought Scripture to my mind, vividly and unmistakably:

"That I may know Him, and the power of His resurrection, and the fellowship of His sufferings, being made conformable unto His death, if that by any means I might attain unto the resurrection of the dead."

I tried to work it out.

"That I may know Him . . ." Yes, I knew that Elberta had not only come to know God, but that during the last three years of her life she had pressed closer and closer to know Him better. Her whole life had been taken up into the effort to know Him better.

"The power of His resurrection . . ." We had all been aware of this in a tremendous new way since the renewing experience of the Holy Spirit. Elberta had experienced the resurrection power even in her physical body, in greatly increased vigour, less need of sleep, and increased blood count, just as the Apostle Paul said:

"If the same Spirit Who raised Christ from the dead dwells in you, He . . . will give new life to your dying bodies . . ." [4]

"The fellowship of His sufferings . . ." Ah, there was the sticking-point! Did anyone truly want that? What was the real meaning of these words?

One thing I knew—when the word "suffering" was used in

the New Testament it didn't mean what we mean by the word today. When we say we "suffer," we usually signify that we are hurt, or have pain, but the Bible word always means: "To put up with something voluntarily." If you *have* to do it, it isn't really a "suffering." I knew that the Apostle Paul was saying something like:

"I willingly put up with all kinds of hardship, even death itself, rather than stop telling about Jesus." And even more profoundly, "rather than stop trusting Jesus implicitly for every need of my life," for to the world this is the deepest offence of the gospel, that we trust God instead of man.

I turned a corner in my walking. The sun, which had been hiding his morning face behind a long roll of clouds concealing the eastern mountains, now began to glint through. It looked as though it would be a fine day. I pursued my thoughts as I pushed on

"The fellowship of His sufferings" then, was something that God's people were supposed to live day by day, and Elberta had certainly done this. She, together with the rest of us, had endured scorn for the sake of Jesus, and had left her home and moved to a faraway city she had never seen. She had gone along with me without flinching when I had resigned my prosperous church, and had expressed no fear at the prospect that my career might come to an end suddenly in the middle of what should have been my most productive years. Elberta had met God in a new fullness; she knew what she had, and what it was worth. She was a faithful witness and, in her quiet way, a strong one.

Yet it was difficult to see how her sickness could be called a part of the "*fellowship* of His sufferings," for Jesus was never sick, and it is impossible to think of Him as being sick. Then, too, sickness is involuntary. The sick person does not take his sickness willingly, and it would be wrong if he did. Rather he attempts to get rid of it: by doctors and medicine; by change of climate or diet; by prayer. No one really questions but that sickness comes from the devil, for if it came from God, how would we dare to seek to be cured?

Elberta did not accept her sickness. She never stopped praying for and expecting healing. When she had put the situation in God's hands at the time of her first surgery, this did not mean that she accepted the sickness, it just meant that she was going to trust God implicitly for her healing. When she decided after her second surgery to accept no more medical treatment, and then refused to take painkillers or drugs, she was not surrendering to the disease, but putting her whole trust in God.

"Why did she died prematurely? Did God refuse to heal her?" Impossible. I knew that if Jesus had come into her room, she would have asked Him, and He would have healed her instantly and completely. As for death, I recall that someone once said:

"Jesus Christ was the world's worst funeral director! He broke up every funeral He ever attended, including His own!" And I know that Jesus was the perfect image of His Father, and did only the things He saw His Father do. All these things about Jesus had to be of the Father, too.

"But God is all-powerful; why did He not heal? God can do anything." We forget that God has limited Himself in one way as far as man is concerned; He has given man free will, and will not overrule our decisions. We are the ones who unconsciously put up blocks to God's power. I have little idea what such blocks might have been in Elberta's case—to speculate would be fruitless—but one thing I do know is that it was not a lack of trust in God on her part. All I know is that for some reason or reasons, the enemy was able to press in and attempt to bring about her death by disease which he and he alone causes, but in this he failed utterly and totally; for God, after letting her fight a brief battle and gain her victory, "took her away . . . by a stroke" as the Scriptures had told me—that is, "in a moment." God did not "take her away" by means of the illness, nor by death—for death, too, is Satan's thing—He took her away *from* illness, from pain, from death, into the glory of His Kingdom. Since her healing was blocked by causes unknown to us, God did what was for her a greater thing, although far harder for us to take: He brought her home! He saw that her life had reached a peak of love and grace, and that there was much "evil to come" for the world, and said:

"The next series of battles is not for you. You have done your work and I'm bringing you home."

As I went up the walk to our little white house on Jones Avenue, the sun was much higher now and comfortingly warm on my back; I felt that some things in this puzzle were fitting into place. It would be a while before I could come to terms all the way, but it was no longer a complete riddle to me.

I went into the house, and sitting down in my study, rested my eyes on Elberta's picture. God's words were certainly true. Yes, she was great in His Kingdom because she walked faithfully in life and in death. The ache in my heart was diminished by the knowledge that God had given her the "crown of life" which He promises to all those who are "faithful unto death."

16
Missionary Rector

Though I was struggling to understand the sorrowful happening in my own life, God did not stop opening doors and giving me assignments. I discovered what many others who had been baptized in the Holy Spirit have discovered, and that is, no matter what doubts and reservations were in my mind, when I stood up to testify to what the Lord was doing, I found myself speaking out with a conviction that I did not know was there! Indeed, sometimes I would feel like a hypocrite; yet it was not hypocrisy, but was the truth in my spirit overriding the doubt in my soul.

It was a chilly autumn Sunday later that year. I had just completed the celebration of the Lord's Supper at our family service. My assistant minister had been "serving" for me, and was standing at the end of the altar with water and wine, assisting me with the "ablutions," the ceremonial cleansing of the communion vessels.

"Ed," I whispered, as he poured the water over my fingers into the chalice, "isn't that the Bishop of Alaska out there?"

Ed looked round quickly. "Yes," he said, "I believe it is!"

The bishop had come, in non-clerical garb, to see for himself what went on at St. Luke's! After the service we renewed our acquaintance at the coffee hour.

"Dennis," he said, putting down his cup, "I'd like to invite you to come to Alaska again so more of my clergy can meet you."

So it was that in January 1964 I went back to Fairbanks, only this time, at 38° below, it was a fairyland completely sheathed in sparkling frost: the midwinter days very short, but very beautiful. It was a contrast to my last visit, which had been in midsummer, when the sun had dipped only briefly below the horizon and one could take snapshots even at midnight!

I went out to the Arctic coast, to Kotzebue, a large village situated on a sand-spit separating the frozen ocean from a frozen lagoon, 7° below, with a brisk 20-knot gale blowing! Here I met my first Eskimos—a people that I quickly came to love and appreciate. Here too I began to experience some of the rigours of missionary life, as I shared with the vicar and his wife, Bobby and Judy, their three-room vicarage, a little bigger, it is true, than most of the Eskimo one-room huts, but utterly devoid of such everyday conveniences as plumbing (of any kind whatever, indoor or outdoor!), running water, or even safe drinking water. I went with Bobby out to the ice lakes behind the town on the dog sled, where chunks of frozen lake water are cut out, brought back, thawed, and the water boiled before it is safe for drinking. I found that for nine months of the year, a bath was a well-nigh unheard-of luxury, unless one was fortunate enough to be invited to the home of a government or school employee who luxuriated in indoor plumbing and hot running water. In the Arctic, an invitation to "dinner and a shower," is perfectly valid, and highly prized!

The night I was to give my testimony, the little Pentecostal Church of God across town closed its own prayer meeting and came to share with us, and I felt far from home in the little corrugated iron building (since replaced with a handsome wooden church) that housed the congregation of "St. George's-in-the-Arctic," my homesickness was tempered as I looked out over a sea of Eskimo faces and saw the familiar glow of those who had been baptized in the Holy Spirit.

That week, too, I met Charlie, a vigorous man in his early seventies, and a much respected leader in the Eskimo community and in the church. Charlie's wife, Lucy, had been quite ill, and Vicar Bob and I went to call and to pray. Another new experience faced me as we walked into their little home, for there was a seal thawing out in the kitchen area, ready for skinning and butchering! After we had prayed with Lucy, I turned to her husband. His love for the Lord seemed obvious.

"Do you know about the Holy Spirit?" I inquired.

"Oh, yes!" he replied, with an infectious smile. "I go down beach. I see seal. I kill seal. I very happy! Holy Spirit fill me!" He gestured expressively.

"Have you ever spoken in tongues?" I inquired.

Charlie shrugged. "I get tongue caught in teeth," he said, seriously. "Talk funny!"

I came back to Anchorage, which looked like a very big city indeed, and then out to amazing Kodiak Island, and back again to Anchorage and on to Seldovia, Juneau, Petersburg, Wrangell, Ketchikan.

The bishop did everything possible to put me in touch with as many of his missionaries as he could—actually I met twenty-three out of thirty-one and a number of these received the Holy Spirit. I also found several who had been speaking in tongues for some time without fully realizing what it meant.

"Dennis," said the pastor of one church, as we came into his house after a meeting, "I think I've been doing something like what you're talking about."

"What do you mean?" I inquired, pulling off my huge fur-lined mitts, and beginning to struggle out of my parka. (Boy, it was cold outside, and good to be in the house!)

"Well, I've a kind of special language that I've used in my prayers for years. I'd never said anything to anyone about it. I guess I thought it was kind of silly, but it always seemed to help me somehow." He sat down on the arm of a chair, and was silent for a second. "Do you think it could be 'speaking in tongues'?"

I was smiling—I had heard this sort of thing before and thought I knew the answer.

"Let's pray," I said, sitting down across the room, "and you pray in this language of yours."

My friend hesitated, then closed his eyes, and after a few halting syllables, began to speak fluently in a beautiful dialect.

"There's no doubt about that!" I said, as he stopped. "Praise God!" It wasn't only the beautiful language that convinced me, it was the refreshing presence of the Holy Spirit which I know we both felt.

This was my longest "missionary journey" thus far. It seemed strange as I returned to Seattle to realize that I had made some good friends in that remote outpost separated from me by thousands of miles of icy water, and frozen tundra.

That same year of 1964 was saddened for us all by the death of the Rt. Rev. William Fisher Lewis, D.D., the man who had originally opened the door to my coming to Seattle and St. Luke's. Bishop Lewis had never wavered in his support of our work, indeed he had shown deep personal interest.

"When are some more churches going to begin doing what yours is doing?" he asked me, on one occasion. He attended a Tuesday night "prayer and praise" meeting back in 1962.

"How did you like it?" I asked him, in a little trepidation.

"It was fine!" he grinned at me. "You rather wore me out,

though. I don't attend many prayer meetings that last three hours!"

During the last few months of his life, he visited meetings at St. Luke's on three occasions. In his last illness, few were allowed to visit him, but he said to me:

"We've been through a lot together, Dennis, and you're not going to be shut out now." He gave orders that I should be allowed to call on him and bring him Holy Communion. His victory in Christ was so evident during this time, that his doctor said to me one day:

"I've never seen anything like it. Every time this man is awake, he has this broad and happy smile on his face!" And Bishop Lewis himself said:

"Dennis, I'm so filled with joy, I hardly know what to do!"

His death brought a new bishop into office, the Rt. Rev. Ivol I. Curtis, who had been assistant Suffragan Bishop of Los Angeles during the crisis at St. Mark's. There were many in the Diocese who wondered what the attitude of the new bishop would be towards the "Charismatic Episcopalians." Bishop Curtis was an old friend—we had been fellow-Rectors in the Diocese of Los Angeles, before his election to the Episcopate —and very shortly after his arrival in Seattle, he took me to lunch, and told me:

"I have found Bishop Lewis to be one of the most wonderful people I have worked with, and I just want you to know, Dennis, that my attitude toward you and your work will be just the same as his." Bishop Curtis, too, has been as good as his word, and not only has given us encouragement at St. Luke's in many ways, but has often given me recommendation to other Bishops, when in my travels I needed such.

But my next adventure was to take me yet further afield than my last. I had been hearing about the "Fountain Trust," a group of ministers and laymen in England who had banded

*"Fountain Trust"
in England*

together to give responsible leadership to what was now being called throughout the world the "Charismatic renewal."* The Rev. Michael Harper, a priest of the Church of England, was on the staff of All Soul's, Langham Place, a London Church which with its Rector, The Rev. John R. W. Stott, has long been a focus of evangelical zeal. Michael had felt called to leave parish work and spend full time with the Fountain Trust as its executive secretary. Under his Spirit-led guidance, this work had already achieved a good deal toward getting English Christians, and especially Anglicans, to understand the revival. Michael and his wife Jeanne visited us early in 1965, and quickly endeared themselves to the Christian fellowship at St. Luke's. They extended to me an invitation to come to England that very summer, and I accepted. This would be my first visit to the land of my birth since I had left it as a boy of nine.

Although I had travelled to the four corners of the United States, this was my first flight overseas, and I was excited as I checked in at the international area at Kennedy Airport, clutching my passport.

"Pan American Flight Two," came the announcement, "London, Frankfurt, Beirut, Teheran!" Even though I was deplaning at the first stop, I felt a vicarious thrill in knowing the big jet on which I was to ride was going to other exotic ports of call—Bangkok, Hong Kong, Tokyo—right around the world and back to the U.S.A. via Honolulu! Minutes later I was walking on board the aircraft. The door to the pilot's cabin was open, and my feeling of adventure quickened at the sight of the sextant mounted in the roof, and the realization that we

---

* "Charismatic" comes from the Greek *charismata,* which means "gifts of love." It is used in the New Testament of the gifts of the Holy Spirit. "Charismatic renewal" means a renewal of these gifts in the Church.

would be travelling where it might be needed, far from the ordinary land facilities of air navigation.

It didn't seem very long before we were landing at London's Heathrow Airport, and I saw Michael and Jeanne waiting to convey me to their interesting flat at the corner of Harley and New Cavendish Streets.

"Why do you call it a flat?" I asked breathlessly of Michael, as we were struggling my suitcases up the fourth flight of stairs to the Harper's apartment.

Michael chuckled. "I suppose it is a little 'vertical' for a flat," he admitted. "A marriage counselling service has the two floors below, while we occupy the three above!"

I found that it was indeed so. One ascended from the street by three flights of winding stairs to the kitchen and living room, while the bedrooms were distributed between the two floors above that! There was little need for jogging to keep exercised in those quarters! I was soon ensconced in a cosy little bedroom at the top of this castle, which was to be my headquarters while I was in England.

I had no sooner established this base of operations than I was whisked off to Cambridge University, where I was to spend a week, and introduced to the Rev. Simon Barrington-Ward, at that time Dean of Chapel of Magdalen College.* I was feeling a little travel weary as we brought my things into the guest room at Magdalen, where I was to stay, and was not particularly cheered by the visage of old Samuel Pepys looking at me darkly from the mantelpiece! I didn't have much time to be concerned about that famous diarist, however; in fact I didn't even have time to inspect his diary, which is a part of the treasures of the library at Magdalen. I found myself busy day and night. I spoke to many faculty and student groups, ad-

---

* "Magdalen," for reasons known to the English, is pronounced "Maudlin"—American readers, please note!

dressed the chaplains of the University, and preached in several of the Anglican churches in Cambridge.

The Rector of Great St. Mary's, the University Church of Cambridge, had written asking if I would speak at the Sunday 11 o'clock service on October 24, and take as my topic:

"Is it decent to speak in tongues?"

I suspect that his own tongue was tucked in his cheek when he wrote this to me! A very short time before my departure for England, however, I had received a second and hasty note from the Rector, saying that he had just realized that October the 24th was designated a "United Nations Sunday," and moreover that the Mayor and Corporation of the City of Cambridge were to make an official visit to the church on that day, and would I please change my topic to:

"Pentecost and the United Nations"?!!

So on that Sunday I looked out at a packed church over a sea of gold maces, scarlet gowns, wigs and cocked hats, where the Mayor and his *entourage* were seated immediately in front of the pulpit. I tried to show that peace among the nations could not come until we had begun to take Jesus' offer seriously that He would give us His peace, and that this, like other gifts of God, came only through a personal acceptance of that same Jesus, and through the work of the Holy Spirit.

The Provost of Southwark Cathedral (pronounced "sutherk"), the Very Rev. Ernest Southcott, was an old friend. When he heard I was to be in England, he invited me to preach at the Cathedral. It was a moving and impressive service. A freestanding altar had been placed at the crossing of the stately old Gothic building, and there the Holy Communion was offered by five concelebrating ministers, assisted by laymen, who brought the bread and the wine down the aisle at offertory time. I spoke on the power of God, and asked the question:

"We have been marching up and down the aisles of this

ancient church building with great enthusiasm, carrying crosses, torches, banners, and singing the militant hymns of the faith. It's grand and inspiring! Outside the doors of this cathedral is the forbidding griminess of this part of London's industrial area on the South Bank of the Thames, the docks, the slums. Are we going to march out of this church into the city outside with the same kind of confidence with which we march around in the church? Where are the people of God going to get the power to show the rescuing love of God in the world outside?" I tried to give the answer to my question. "By the acceptance of Jesus the Saviour and by the release of the Holy Spirit in and through our lives—by a renewal of the experience of Pentecost!"

I spoke at four of the major theological colleges of the Church of England—Westcott, Ridley, Cuddesdon, and the London College of Divinity. In each I was courteously received, and in all but one, virtually the entire faculty and student body was there to hear what I had to say. My testimony was received with real and deep interest. I came to realize that one of my main tasks on this trip was to help "unhook" some of the "hang-ups" which hamper theologians in their understanding of the Baptism in the Holy Spirit.

The Bishops of Bedford, Southwark, and Coventry all invited me to address them and their clergy, and I was really delighted with the openness that I found there, too. Neither in the theological schools nor from the clergy did I receive any unfriendly or ungracious challenges, although there were, of course, urgent questions.

The chapter meeting of the Coventry clergy was held in the little village of Offchurch, in the old rectory, which had been made into a chapter house. We met in the morning with thirty or so of the clergy who were working in "high-density" areas of the diocese. The Rev. Stephen Verney, well-known for his book, *Fire in Coventry*, a story of the spiritual revival centre-ing around the building of the new cathedral after the old one had been almost totally destroyed in World War II, chaired the meeting, and I told once again of the great things God was doing in my own country and other parts of the world. After luncheon the bishop arrived, the Rt. Rev. Cuthbert Bardsley, prepared to lead a business session, but the men said to him:

"My Lord Bishop, we would like to have more dialogue with our visitor about the work of the Holy Spirit. Would that be in order?"

And the Bishop replied with a beaming smile:

"That's exactly what I would like to do!" So we had another couple of hours of good sharing. The bishop wrote later to Michael:

"I would like to thank you and Father Bennett very warmly indeed for your great kindness in coming to Offchurch last week. It was exactly what we all needed, and I came away tremendously encouraged and grateful for your contribution . . ."

I was also invited to speak at the Ecumenical House at Oxford University, where the well-known Russian scholar and churchman, Dr. Nicholas Zernov, was chairman of the meeting; then, returning to London, David DuPleiss and I found ourselves as luncheon guests of a group of the leading evangelicals of England, both Anglican and Non-conformist. I was delighted with their openness and freedom from prejudice, especially that peculiarly American doctrine of extreme "dispensationalism"—"These things are not for today!"—which is so often the defence of the stateside evangelical. Another contact with the heart of English evangelical Christianity came when I spoke at Westminster Chapel, where Dr. Martyn Lloyd-Jones has pastored for many years. The meeting was sponsored by the Fountain Trust, but Dr. Lloyd-Jones attended, and afterwards I enjoyed a warm and encouraging conversation with him. The Dean of Wesminster Abbey, the Very Rev. Eric Abbott, asked Michael Harper and me to come and see him, and we spent a good hour in his study adjoining the Abbey. He, too, was genuinely interested. All in all, it was a fruitful and action-packed time.

Although my main ministry on this trip was teaching, many received the Holy Spirit, and some were delivered from sickness or other oppressions of the enemy. I won't soon forget two striking things that happened at an interchurch meeting in a London suburb. We had met in the social hall of the Methodist Church, and after the main session, a small group had gathered in an upstairs classroom to hear more about the Baptism in the Holy Spirit. Michael Harper was with me. After making sure that all present had personally accepted Jesus Christ as their Saviour, I began to pray for those who asked—a few for healing, or other needs, but mostly praying for them to receive the Holy Spirit. Once again the miracle began to happen, as Christians, already indwelt by the Holy Spirit, began to trust Jesus to inundate them with His power and freedom, so that the riches stored in them could break forth to the world. One after another, some hesitantly, some fluently, they began to speak in new languages.

I came to a young lady with bright red hair sitting expectantly on the edge of her chair, eyes closed in prayer. As I laid my hands on her head and asked Jesus to baptize her in the Holy Spirit, she began to speak. It was obvious from her general appearance that she was not a well educated person, probably a worker in one of the nearby factories. She began immediately and effortlessly to speak in a beautiful and flowing language that was obviously not her own. Everyone stopped and listened. She began very softly, with her head bowed, then lifted her head and her voice. We all knew she was praying and praising God, and the sense of His Presence was very real and sweet. After a few more moments she again dropped her head, began to speak more softly—then stopped. Her hands were lying open in her lap, and her eyes were still closed in prayer. Prompted, I am sure, by the Holy Spirit, I said to her:

"My dear, you can interpret what you have just said!" Ordinarily I would not have encouraged such interpretation, for the kind of "speaking in tongues" that takes place at the time of receiving the baptism in the Holy Spirit is the beginning of the "prayer tongue" which is going to be used in private devotion, and needs no interpretation. It is "speaking to God in a mystery," as Paul says. In this case, however, I felt that God wanted this girl to interpret her speaking, so that we could all share in the blessing.

Without a moment's hesitation, she began to interpret, that is, to bring in English the meaning of her speaking. I cannot remember her words to quote them in detail, except that they were a beautiful and childlike prayer to God. As she interpreted, she began softly with her head bowed, then raised her head and her voice, just as she had done while speaking in tongues, and concluded again by dropping her head and her tone. It was utterly artless, and utterly convincing. Several people in the room were openly wiping tears from their eyes.

I moved on round the room, and in my praying came to a young man whose face was drawn and white; he looked completely depressed and distressed. I put forward my hand to pray for him, but before I could touch him, he was literally thrown from his chair on to the floor. I realized he was being tormented by demonic power, so I rebuked the evil spirit at once, bound it under the Blood of Jesus, and cast it out in the Name of Jesus, never to return. The young man immediately calmed down and climbed back into his chair, but I could see that he was still very agitated. It startled me to see that the whites of his eyes were blood-red from the violence of his ordeal! I said to my companion:

"Would you take this man into the next room and pray for him further?"

Those who went with him told me later that the whole performance was repeated, and another tormenting spirit cast out. After that, the young man happily received the Holy Spirit!

I felt that it was God's wisdom that led the young lady to give such an undoubted manifestation of the beauty and validity of the gift of tongues in order to prepare those in the room for the second, rather shattering, experience. As it was, no one was disturbed, and a number of others also received their Pentecost, but none looked more radiant than the young man who had been so dramatically set free from bondage.

17
A New Chapter

Nearly three years had gone by since Elberta's home-going. During those years I had had no problem keeping busy. I had given my testimony over and over again, not only at home in our Friday night meeting, but throughout the United States and overseas, telling of the release of God's life in people as they received the Baptism in the Holy Spirit. For me on a personal level though, they had been dry and lonely years. I was having difficulty keeping any kind of spiritual joy and freedom, and there were times when, as I told again of my experience, it seemed I was only talking of a memory. It was not surprising that I should feel this way, although I certainly did not understand it at the time. Here I was, entertaining all kinds of doubts and fears and even resentment toward God, because of my great personal loss—behaving with the exact opposite of faith —and yet expecting to be able to enjoy His fellowship at the same time. He hadn't left me, of course, but how could He possibly show Himself to me, when I had my back turned toward Him? Friendship is a two-way street; you cannot at the same time be questioning the goodness of a friend, and also enjoying his love and fellowship, and it isn't any different if that Friend happens to be the Lord! Not fully understanding these things, I almost felt that I had come to the end of my story, and all the while God was waiting for me to trust him, so that He could begin a new chapter.

One Friday night in mid-March of 1966, as I opened the "instruction" meeting at St. Luke's and prepared for the many-hundredth time to give my testimony to the waiting people, my eyes spied an unexpected visitor in the congregation—Rita Reed.

I had known Rita casually for some five years off and on. We had met briefly in the summer of 1961 at the Full Gospel Businessmen's Fellowship International Convention in Miami. Her brother, William Standish Reed, a well-known Christian surgeon, widely hailed in charismatic circles, had introduced us. Both Dr. Bill and I were to be speakers at the convention. On a Sunday morning a group of us went to an Episcopal Church for an early morning communion service, had a pleasant visit over breakfast, and then went to a Full Gospel church service—a truly ecumenical morning! I remembered Rita as an attractive and pleasant young lady, some years younger than I, who obviously loved the Lord Jesus very much.

I had seen her again in 1965 at a convention in Spokane. Mutual friends invited us individually to visit with them in their hotel suite one afternoon, and each of us was surprised to find the other there. It was pleasant to renew the acquaintance and to continue conversation further over dinner. After that visit she sent me a copy of a little book she had prepared for her Bible classes on the gifts of the Holy Spirit, asking me to cast a critical theological eye over it. I found it to be sound, and said so. I had an inclination to get better acquainted with her, but Spokane was three hundred difficult miles away, and I just never found time to make the journey. Now here she was sitting in the parish hall at St. Luke's. I was very pleased to see her.

"Rita!" I greeted her, taking her hand. "How good to see you again!"

"It's nice to see you, too, Father Bennett," she replied with a smile.

"What brings you over Seattle way?"

'Oh," she said, "I was invited to speak for several of the Christian women's clubs in this area, and for some prayer groups, too. Being so close to St. Luke's, I didn't want to miss attending a meeting here."

"Where are you staying?" I inquired.

"With some of your parishioners as a matter of fact, Verle and Chloris," she responded.

It was time for me to open the meeting. "What about coming to speak to the college group tomorrow night? I'll come and get you." I wanted Rita to tell our college people something of the work she was doing with young people in Spokane.

The next night she did come to the meeting, and afterward I took her home. She had never been in Seattle before, and it seemed very logical to give her a little tour of the city—it's especially beautiful at night. As we drove, I asked her about her brother Bill, and others of our mutual friends. Then after a little time of silence, much to my own surprise, I came out flatly with the question:

"Rita, how old are you?"

She looked at me a little surprised, but answered pleasantly enough: "Me? Oh, I'm thirty-two."

Embarrassed by my own impertinence, I lapsed into silence again, but my mind was very busy. *Thirty-two, eh? She's older than I thought she was. Now why should I be thinking like that?*

We stopped at a restaurant for a bite to eat, and then I delivered my guest to the door of the spacious home on Queen Anne Hill. I resisted a strange impulse to kiss her good-night!

I gave myself a "talking-to" on the way home. "Now look here, this young lady is just a friend. Cut out the nonsense! You're going to make a fool of yourself for sure if you don't look out!"

The next day was Sunday, and Rita came to the family church service bringing with her a curly-headed seventeen-year-old by the name of Sibley. I had heard something of this young man. He was from Spokane, and a number of months before he had been run over by a car and terribly injured. Rita had heard of his condition at a home prayer meeting: Fractured skull, brain damage, paralysed on one side, a broken leg which could not be set because of his precarious balance between life and death, gangrene in both feet, in a state of semi-consciousness for a month— It would take a miracle indeed to remedy this young man's condition, but Rita felt led to go and pray with him. At the nursing home, she met Sibley's mother for the first time. Together they, and another friend, went into a room where the boy was lying. He was not a hopeful sight, this once nice-looking teenager: most of his hair had fallen out, his body was mere skin and bones, with tubes carrying out the basic functions of life. His eyes were blank and staring.

The mother broke the silence:

"The doctors tell me that my son cannot communicate with anyone—there has been too much brain damage. I can't quite believe this, though, because when I talk to him, I am sure that he moves his eyebrows in a kind of response."

Rita knew something of this kind of situation. She remembered her brother Bill's experience with a young girl, Karen Emmott, several years before. Karen, too, had been given up as a hopeless case, until God intervened.* She knew her brother believed that even in a coma, a patient could often know and

* Catherine Marshall, *Beyond Ourselves* (McGraw-Hill, 1961), pp. 221–228.

understand everything that was said to him or her, even though unable to respond. She had a sudden inspiration, and taking Sibley by the hand, spoke to him:

"If Jesus heals you, Sibley, will you live for Him? If your answer is 'yes,' squeeze my hand three times."

What was her excitement to feel one—two—three definite squeezes of her hand! Without doubt Sibley had heard and understood every word! With this sign that a miracle of healing was already beginning, Rita now with even greater confidence prayed with the prayer of faith, the others agreeing in prayer with her:

"Father, I thank You for what You have already done, and in Jesus' Name I ask You to restore Your child and make him whole again."

Next day the nurse noticed Sibley moving his head, and seeming more alert. He then proceeded to pull out the tube through which he was being fed directly into his stomach. His nurse decided to try giving him some Jello, and he gobbled it down avidly! She tried a cookie, and that disappeared just as quickly! It wasn't long before the nurse realized she was trying to fill the void in a teenager who hadn't eaten for a solid month! Soon the boy was talking, recognizing people, and eating quite normally. The doctors, being told of Sibley's sudden improvement, brought him back from the nursing home to the hospital to see what they might do further to help him. It was during this time that Rita, arrayed in a sterilized hospital gown, prayed with Sibley to receive the Holy Spirit! Soon this young man, who a few short weeks previously had been considered a hopeless case, unable to communicate at all, was praising God in a new language, given by the Holy Ghost! Not long after this, he was back at home, and on the way to an amazing recovery.

It was a real joy to see Sibley in church that morning, and to realize again the power of God—the power which we limit so pitifully. On the way out of church, I greeted them and asked Rita:

"How much longer will you be in the Seattle area?"

"A few more days," she replied. "By the way, Father Bennett, do you have anyone in the parish who could help me counsel with a woman who is deeply depressed?"

I gave her the name of a long-time Bible teacher, known as Aunt Ada to more than one generation of Christians! Ada, brought up as a Lutheran in Sweden, and later as a good fundamental Baptist, had received the Baptism in the Holy Spirit. To my great delight she had joined our congregation, bringing her strong teaching ministry into our fellowship. Although getting on in years physically, she was young in spirit, and many St. Lukans profited by her teaching and wisdom.

They made contact, and Rita was invited to dinner the next day, but when she arrived at Ada's pleasant little home on Phinney Ridge, her hostess said with a motherly twinkle:

"I hope you won't mind, but I've invited Father Bennett to join us for dinner at the 'Windjammer'!"

That evening as we sat together across the table from Ada, more than once during the meal I found myself glancing at the young lady by my side. How nice to have her there!

18
"Two are Better than One"

When I returned from my second journey to Alaska, I had found my older son waiting to talk to me. He was very excited.

'Hey Dad, I've found out what I want to be!" he said. "I want to be an airline pilot. We've been down to the airport while you were gone, and found out that it'll cost only about $3,000 to get the training I'll need!"

I looked quizzically at my son. "Only $3,000, eh?" I said. "And where are you going to get *that* kind of money?" Steve was at the in-between stage of not yet settling on what he wanted to do with his life, and I thought that this might be a "flash in the pan"—but I was wrong. Steve did manage to finance his project, and before long was on his way to becoming a very fine light plane pilot.

I had been flying on big aircraft for a long time and loved every minute of it. While I was in Alaska, a friend had taken me for my first trip in a small plane. We had flown in his Cherokee 160 over the Kenai Peninsula, and into Seldovia. On the way back he had let me "steer" for a while! Now my son said to me:

"Dad, why don't you come on down and take a lesson? You'll like it, I'm sure."

I did, and I was "hooked"! By the end of 1965 I had my private licence, and early in 1966 took the doubtful step of becoming part-owner of "N-8191-Bravo," an elderly Cessna 172, a gentle old girl with a chequered history. I found this new avocation to be not only intriguing and challenging, but also healing. It was a lot of fun, although I didn't know what use it would be in my life; now I began to get a clue.

By the spring of 1966, I had become a fairly proficient pilot, but I had never made the cross-country journey eastward to Spokane. Here was a good excuse for a visit with Rita! On the 2nd of April I wrote to her and said that, weather permitting, I would be flying "91-Bravo" over the Cascades, and what about lunch?

Rita told me later:

"I realized by your decision to fly over to see me, that you were beginning to show more than a brotherly interest! I was flattered; yet I was happy being single, free to go wherever and whenever God directed. I had had opportunities to marry several times in my life, but somehow had never done so. Suppose you wanted to get serious! I had turned my life over to the Lord, and was not at all sure marriage was in His plan for me, even if it was to someone as nice as Dennis Bennett!"

Since it was my first trip east of the mountains in the little plane, I examined my charts carefully and filed my flight plan. Rita had just moved out to a retreat centre called "Living Springs Ranch," so my destination was the Deer Park Airport, fifteen miles northwest of Spokane. I noticed from the chart that although it was quite a small town, it boasted a good-sized airfield, a relic of World War II.

It was a beautiful day. The flight through the Cascades was without incident, and the scenery magnificent. I crossed the

Columbia and then the long dry plain between the Cascades and the Spokane area. As I came over the last range of hills and eased back on the throttle to begin a long glide down from my cruising altitude, I saw the airport dead ahead—looking just as the chart showed it. There were three big runways arranged in a triangle. No sweat! Just a matter of finding out which way the wind was blowing. Setting my radio to the Spokane tower frequency, I picked up the mike:

"Spokane tower, this is Cessna Eight-one-niner-one Bravo. Please close my V.F.R. flight plan to Deer Park, and give me the wind numbers. Over." The controller's response made the rest very simple. The wind was right down runway 22—but one thing puzzled me as I circled over the field: all the tyre marks were at one end of the runway, the *opposite* end from the one I wished to land on! Gave me a kind of funny feeling. According to those skid marks, or rather the lack of them, nobody had landed on that runway in the direction I wanted to land for a long time! Why not? I flew low over the area several times, but could not see any obstacles—could not see any reason why my 172 should not settle down nicely on that piece of concrete. Finally, with more daring than good sense, I swung into a downwind, base, and final approach, and touched the wheels down in a "greaser" that warmed my pilot's heart! No problem yet—but as I taxied to the far end, I discovered it. There was a fence—a good heavy one, too—stretched right across the airstrip, but invisible from the air. And the black tyre marks all at one end? Very simple. This runway had been converted into an automobile "drag strip"!

I taxied over to tie down the airplane and saw Rita waiting for me. After the ship was secured, she came out to greet me.

"You sure had me concerned for a while!" she said. "I didn't know anything about this airport until arriving to wait for you. A man drove by, noticed I was waiting, and said it was quite rare for anyone to land here since two of the runways had become drag strips. 'Drag strip!' I echoed. He drove away and left me wondering: *How in the world can I warn Dennis?* The only answer was to pray, and pray hard!"

"Sure glad you did!" I said, as we walked to her little white Rambler. "*Someone* was looking out for me. If the wind had been from the other direction I would certainly have bent the airplane, to say nothing of myself!"

We drove through the town and down the country road to the retreat centre where Rita was staying, and greeted her good friends and hosts, Dean and Cordie. The picnic lunch on Mt. Zion, as the nearby wooded hill had been christened, was pleasant but brief, for I had to return to Seattle the same afternoon.

It wasn't long before I found another excuse to visit her. This time I flew "commercial," the Cascade weather not being friendly to small aircraft. We took a stroll in the woods in quest of wild flowers and conversation. I offered Rita my arm as we walked—and it was fortunate I did, for on the way down a steep slope she tripped, and would have fallen had she not been able to steady herself.

"Oh," she apologized, a little embarrassed. "That's me! I tend to stumble when I'm going downhill."

It was only about five minutes later that the trail began to climb, and suddenly it was my turn to stumble. This time I was glad that Rita could help me keep on my feet!

"Well," I said, "you may stumble going downhill, but *I* trip over my feet going *up*!" We laughed about it, not thinking it might have meaning for us later on.

"Why don't we sit down here awhile," I said, indicating an inviting patch of green grass.

"Fine," my companion said, suiting the action to the word, as I seated myself beside her.

"Tell me more of your story, Rita."

"I've known Jesus ever since I can remember," she replied thoughtfully, "but I made a personal acceptance of Him at the age of nine, and shortly after this I was baptized with the Holy Spirit. It was quite a dramatic experience. I spoke in tongues for about two hours and prophesied!"

"Now, that's great!" I said. "Wish I'd received the Holy Spirit that early in life!"

"Yes, it should have been great," Rita went on, "only for me it didn't turn out that way. If someone had just told me what to do next, that the Baptism with the Holy Spirit was a *continuing* experience and that I should pray "in the Spirit" —in tongues—every day, it would have been wonderful. As it was, the memory of my experience faded, and as I entered my teens all I recalled was that something embarrassingly "different" had happened to me. I tried to put it out of my mind. At the same time I was chafing at the "thou shalt nots" and began looking for a church that would make fewer demands on me. I tried a variety, and in my senior year at the University of Florida I began to look at the Episcopal Church. Those Episcopalians didn't say much about 'thou shalt nots'; they quoted St. Augustine instead, who said: 'Love God, and do what you please!' It sounded pretty good to me at the time! Later, of course, I was to find that as you love God more and more, you will soon be doing what pleases Him."

I nodded, and she went on:

"I even spent a month, shortly after my graduation, studying in the Episcopal training programme for educators and church workers at Newport, Rhode Island. While there I was offered a job at a church agency in New Jersey, working with needy children.

"My big brother, whom I much admired, had become an Episcopalian some time before. When he heard I was to be confirmed, he wrote reminding me that at the time of confirmation I was supposed to receive the 'strengthening gifts of the Holy Spirit.'[1] Not understanding my childhood experience, I didn't actually know what the 'gifts of the Holy Spirit'[2] were, or if I had ever received any of them. Following confirmation I didn't see any definite change in my life right away, but the bishop's prayer was to be answered in a remarkable way nearly two years later."

Rita interrupted her story. "It's getting a bit chilly," she said, clambering to her feet and offering me her hand. "Let's walk on a little further."

"Seems a lot of us have to be shaken up before we are ready to come to terms with the Lord," she continued. "It was after I had moved back to my hometown of Tampa, Florida, and had gone into social work that I was shaken out of my complacency. I had a dear and close friend who roomed with me, named Gaye Miller. She confided in me one day that she 'spoke in tongues.' This baffled me. The only time I recalled hearing people 'speak in tongues' was in a public meeting, and they seemed extremely emotional and 'worked up.' On the other hand, as I well knew, Gaye had a quietly beautiful life in which the power and presence of God was very evident.

" 'You speak in tongues?' I asked incredulously.

"And Gaye nodded: 'Every day!' she said.

" 'Every day? But how? Where?' Gaye and I had shared the same apartment for over a year. How could she possibly have been 'speaking in tongues' daily without my knowing it? She explained that speaking in tongues need not be loud or demonstrative at all, but that one could have the benefit of praying in the Spirit quietly during his private prayers and often through the day. I was impressed, but still hesitant about getting involved. Shortly after this Gaye had moved to another state, and I did not discuss it with her further.

"Then came the blow. Gaye, while on her lunch hour, was

suddenly stricken with a cerebral haemorrhage. She just had time to give her name and address before dropping into an unconsciousness from which her physical body never returned. She died eight hours later. When I received the news, I was horribly shocked. For several nights I hardly slept. I knew Gaye was in good standing with the Lord, but I had no such confidence about myself. What if I should die suddenly without any chance to make things right with God? I went, still in great distress, to the funeral, and there met for the first time John and Bertha, the couple in whose home Gaye had met with others for prayer each Friday night.

"The next week Bertha phoned me:

" 'While I was praying today,' she said, 'the Lord suddenly began talking to me about *you*!'

"I said nothing for several moments. This was a new way of speaking which I wasn't quite used to, but the wheels were turning in my mind, rapidly. I answered, 'He did?' Then I thought to myself: *I didn't know for sure whether God still knew I was around!*

"My caller said: 'If you'd be interested to know more about it why don't you drop over to my house today?'

"As I hung up the phone I decided to go right over and see what this was all about.

"I was amazed when my new acquaintance shared with me things that she could not have known unless God had told her. (I know now that this is what the Bible calls the gift of knowledge.) As Bertha told what she felt God had said to her, there was a definite response in my own heart. One statement in particular seemed to stick in my mind:

" 'The gifts are at your feet, where you left them!'

"I was planning that Friday night to audition to sing at a club on the Gulf beach near Tampa, but decided, somewhat to my own amazement, to give up this coveted ambition and go to the weekly prayer meeting instead!

"At that meeting I came into contact again with the experience I had left behind in my youth—the Baptism in the Holy Spirit—only this time in a very different setting. Here were members of 'old-line' churches, yet with an obvious new excitement and involvement which they said had come from receiving the Holy Spirit.

"After a time of enthusiastic singing, intercessory prayer, and inspiring testimonies the leader asked: 'Rita, would you like us to pray for you?'

"I thought, *Prayer wouldn't hurt me, I suppose, but—in front of sixty or seventy strangers?! Now if only there were an Episcopal priest here, I would be sure that everything would be conducted in a dignified manner!*

"I consented to be prayed for, however, and the leader called: 'Father Sherry! Come over here, won't you?'

"Could it be? Yes, here came a little man, an Episcopal priest, lovingly known to his many friends as Father Sherry, to pray for me! Seeing the kindly face and twinkling eyes of the elderly minister, I felt more confident. Then I was in for another surprise: when Father Sherry laid his hands on my head and prayed, he didn't speak English, he spoke fluently in a foreign language! As he prayed, the presence of God broke through so greatly that tears began to pour from my eyes, and I suddenly recognized that this Episcopal priest was praying in tongues, in a language given by the Holy Spirit. Almost before I realized it, I too began to praise God in a new language just as I had done sixteen years before. Truly the gifts were at my feet where I'd left them. From that evening on, my life was utterly transformed. Having known what it was like to walk *without* the conscious awareness of God's presence all those years, I now gave my life completely to Him.

"I worked for a while with my brother Bill, who, in addition to practising medicine, travelled and spoke widely to Christian endeavours. Later I spent two years on the staff of *Trinity*."

"That magazine helped a lot of people understand the charismatic renewal, didn't it?" I commented.

Rita nodded. In our walking we had come to a little glen, brimming with black-eyed Susans.

"What brought you to the Northwest?" I asked, as we stopped for a few moments to enjoy the sight.

"I felt the need to spend some time in prayer seeking God's further will for my life," Rita said. "And I was invited to come to Deer Park, where Dean and Cordie were in the initial stages of developing this retreat centre. I had planned to stay two weeks, but they stretched into two years. I was not only able to make my retreat as I'd planned, but also found myself being put to work by the Lord, teaching classes and study groups, and working with young people in the Spokane area. I was also able to receive some excellent instruction myself."

We didn't say much more as we walked the remaining distance to the little white chalet guesthouse at the heart of Living Springs Ranch.

Our friendship grew during our visits back and forth across the state of Washington. Although neither Rita nor I "fell in love at first sight," we both realized more and more that God was drawing us together. On occasion we talked frankly about the possibility of marriage, yet neither of us wanted to make a decision without being certain that it was what God wanted.

In July, Rita was again invited to the coastal area to speak to some women's clubs, and I came to visit at the home in Olympia where she was staying. As soon as we could find a quiet place, I said:

"Rita, I found a most interesting passage of Scripture this

morning. Seems to me it has something to say to us!" Picking up a Bible and opening it, I continued. "Ecclesiastes 4:9–12 goes like this:

"'Two are better than one.'" I paused and glanced at Rita. "'For they have a good reward for their labour. For if they *fall*, the one will lift up his fellow: but woe to him that is alone when he *falleth;* for he hath not another to help him up.'" I paused again, and Rita looked at me and smiled, remembering our hikes in the woods! The reference became more pointed: "'. . . But how can one be warm alone? And if one prevail against him, two shall withstand him, and a threefold cord is not quickly broken.'"

"A threefold cord?" she said. "Sounds like a Christian marriage . . . husband, wife, and Jesus."

"Rita," I said, "I do believe God wants us to walk together, and that He wants us to be married. I know it's what I want. What do you say?"

She looked at me for a moment and then said: "Yes, Dennis, I do want to marry you, but I need to hear from God myself. I'll go home and pray about it for the next three days; then I'll let you know for sure and finally. Okay?"

Those were three long days for me, and I did a lot of tugging at God's sleeve! On the evening of the third day I called Rita:

"Dennis," she said, and my heart skipped a beat, "I just want to tell you that you now have a double 'yes'—once from me, and once from the Lord!"

Before too many days I was again winging my way over the Cascades·in Nine-One-Bravo, only this time it was not just to visit, but to bring my bride-to-be back to Seattle.

My secretary and good friend, Florence, had opened her home to Rita while we began the happy process of getting her better acquainted with my family and friends. One day Rita said:

"Dennis, I would like to go to the cemetery with some flowers for Elberta's grave." She added: "You know, I don't want or expect you to forget Elberta. Her memory is a part of you. I want you to feel free to talk about her so I can grow to love her too!"

If there were any reservations left in my heart about the rightness of remarrying, they were at this time put to rest.

When was the wedding to take place? I had been invited to go to New Zealand for three weeks in September.

"Sounds like a good idea for a honeymoon!" I suggested to Rita.

She looked doubtful. "Uh, how many speaking engagements do you have in those three weeks?" she inquired.

"Oh, let's see—fifty-seven at the last count, I think."

Rita smiled sweetly. "I think, Dennis," she said slowly, "that it wouldn't be such a good idea for a honeymoon! Tell you what—" she continued, "I'd love to see New Zealand, but this doesn't seem to be the time. I want to spend a few weeks with my family, so why don't you go to New Zealand, while I go to Tampa and get things ready for the wedding?"

It did make sense, although I hated to part for what I knew would seem much longer than three weeks. Reluctantly, I put Rita on the plane for Florida; then a few days later, I left on my journey to the South Pacific.

19
"Signs Following"

I climbed aboard a Boeing 720 around supper time, flying from
Seattle to San Francisco, and then, with a change of planes, on
to Honolulu. A brief stopover at 10 p.m. in the Paradise of the
Pacific, and on to Nandi, in the Fiji Islands. A few more hours
in the stratosphere—with as little sensation of travel as one
might have sitting in the living room at home—and it was
dawn; we were approaching Auckland, New Zealand. It didn't
take long for me to see that it was a very beautiful country,
somehow magically blending the rugged beauty of the Pacific
Northwest with the tropical softness of the Caribbean.

I learned that the Polynesian discoverers of New Zealand
named it "Aotearoa," the "Land of the Long White Cloud,"
because their first indication of the islands as they voyaged in
their canoes were the long stratus clouds hovering over them.
When I first arrived at Auckland, however, and for several days
thereafter, it seemed rather to be the "land of the long black
cloud," for I had arrived in the midst of the spring rains! It
reminded me of home!

I was met at the Auckland Airport by the rector of St.
Paul's parish, The Venerable Kenneth R. Prebble, a gracious

Englishman who is also archdeacon of Hauraki. On our way to his home where I was to stay during my first weekend in his country, he said:

"I don't know whether I can accept this 'Baptism with the Holy Spirit' you're talking about, Dennis."

"How did you come to be interested in it at all?" I inquired.

"That's a long story," the archdeacon replied. "A number of months ago a young man, a successful clothing manufacturer in Auckland, said he was led by the Holy Spirit to come into my church, St. Paul's, one day during the week—he didn't exactly know why. He approached me and opened a conversation in what struck me as being rather a brash manner. As I recall, he asked me why I had no tracts about salvation in the tract rack!"

I chuckled. "Not the smoothest approach in the world," I commented.

"No," agreed the archdeacon dryly, "it wasn't. As a matter of fact, I was really quite nasty to the young man. Tried to get rid of him, you know! But he wouldn't go—followed me into my office. I had no choice but to offer him a cup of coffee, and we somehow got into conversation about this business of 'receiving the Holy Spirit' and 'speaking in tongues.' I probably wouldn't have listened at all, except that my curiosity had already been aroused. A short time before this I had come into the church one day and found a woman quietly praying out loud in a foreign language. I asked her:

"'Were you speaking in tongues a moment ago?'

"She said, 'Yes, I was, as a matter of fact.'

"She seemed very normal and well-balanced. Then of course, I'd been hearing some other reports from here and there.

"Anyway, my bold young friend went on to tell me of a prayer meeting that was being held weekly in a private home, and invited me to attend. To my own amazement, and I'm sure to his also, I went!"

I whistled softly. "What happened then?"

"One part of me was shocked to the core, of course," he confided, in his clipped, quiet English manner. "But the other part was tremendously moved. I'd never been where people were praying and sharing so freely. The informality of it backed me off a bit, but on the other hand, I knew immediately that there was genuine holiness there—God was there! I went back the next week, and took my wife with me. She liked it right away!"

The archdeacon brought his little car to a halt outside a white porticoed house that proclaimed by a small signboard: St. Paul's Rectory. Across the street was the church—quite a large building in a rather elaborate Victorian Gothic style. I cast an apprehensive eye at the weather—it was pouring rain. Before we got out of the car, my new acquaintance finished his story.

"We've been to this meeting now a number of times. I've never seemed fully able to take part, though. Seems as though there is a part of me that is still frozen solid! But I do benefit from going.

"Then," he concluded, "a few weeks ago two very junior clergy of this area called on me. 'We hear you are going to this charismatic prayer meeting,' they said, with happy candour. I thought to myself: *The cat's out of the bag, for sure!* but I admitted yes, I had. 'Well,' they said, 'if you're interested in this matter of the Baptism in the Holy Spirit, we thought you'd like to know that Dennis Bennett is coming to New Zealand very soon.'

"I was quite surprised about your coming and wanted to know who was sponsoring you. I had heard a tape of your testimony a few weeks before, and rather liked it, but invitations to overseas' clergy visitors usually come down through accepted channels, and neither the bishop nor I had heard anything about your coming. The young men named the assistant minister at a parish in one of the smaller cities as the person who was setting up the tour. Then they asked if I would sponsor you in Auckland and clear you with the Bishop here! I thought it was a clear case of the tail wagging the dog, but I consented. The Bishop wasn't too pleased at first, but when he received a fine letter from your Bishop Curtis telling us some good things about you, affirming that you were in 'good and regular' standing, he gave his consent."

My friend unbuckled his seat belt and opened the car door. I followed suit. He paused and looked at me with a grin:

"So that's how I found myself sponsoring this questionable character from the U.S.A.!" he said. We both ran for the house through the pelting rain.

I was still sleeping soundly the next morning when the archdeacon arose, as was his custom, and went across the street to say his morning prayers in the church. Again the miracle happened: while he was praying, his words suddenly changed, and he began to pray strongly in a new language. He was overwhelmed with the joy and power of the Spirit!

I was scheduled to spend the day at Gisborne, a little town on the eastern coast of the North Island, about one hundred miles away, and to return that night to make my first public address at St. Matthew's Church in downtown Auckland, so it was with considerable anxiety that I found, when I arrived at the airport for my return plane, that the flight was indefinitely delayed due to weather. I sat in the Gisborne airport and watched the time of the meeting in Auckland approach, and then pass by: 7.30, 8.00, 8.30—and finally the airplane arrived. I felt in my spirit that the Lord had a purpose in this delay—but did not guess what!

I walked into the meeting at St. Matthew's at 9.30 p.m. to find a tremendously enthusiastic group of people. Obviously they hadn't been waiting for me! What had happened? The archdeacon told me about it later.

"We were very distressed when we discovered that we had a crowd of some two hundred people, and no speaker," he said. "And the other committee members just didn't know what to do! When I spoke in tongues this morning, I thought, *Well now, I'd better keep this quiet, I'd better not tell anyone about it for a while, as they might not understand.* But tonight, when I realized that you were not going to get here in time for the meeting, I knew that I was supposed to get up and tell what happened to me. So I did!"

And what a sensation it made in the Anglican Church, not just in Auckland, but the length and breadth of the country!

Later that first week I had a meeting with the Bishop of Auckland and members of the clergy. Hearing of the archdeacon's experience had certainly brought the clergy out in full force. In introducing me, he said:

"My Lord Bishop and brethren, I just want to say to you that I am in full agreement with this man in what he is saying."

In the meantime, I had been thoroughly enjoying my stay at the rectory. The rector's wife, Mary, had been most hospitable, but what did she think about it? She hadn't said a word, pro or con. Was she glad about what had happened to her husband? Later that first week we had taken a day off and gone to Manley Beach, where my friends had a little cottage. The weather was not conducive to bathing or beaching, so we had just been taking it easy in the house in front of a cheerful fire, chatting about many things. Mary had been listening to our talk, dropping a remark here and there; but suddenly she stood up, excused herself, and went outside. She was gone for some little time, then returned, with a broad smile on her face.

"Well," she reported, "I can do it all right! The only problem is that I don't want to stop!" She had gone out into the garden, asked Jesus to baptize her in the Holy Spirit, and after a few moments of prayer, had begun to speak fluently in a new language!

I left Auckland at the end of the week, and travelled pretty much the length and breadth of New Zealand. I spoke to bishops and clergy in the dioceses of Christchurch, Dunedin, and Wellington. I addressed faculty and students at the two Anglican theological colleges, and spoke also to a big gathering of students at Massey University in Palmerston North, where about five per cent of the entire student body had received the Baptism in the Holy Spirit as a result of the witness of the Anglican chaplain, who was the man who had set up my trip in the first place.

As always, there were interesting contacts and "signs following." In a beautiful little seacoast town on the South Island, the Anglican vicar had planned a meeting, and a goodly number turned out to hear the visiting American. As we sat waiting for the evening to begin, my host seemed a little uneasy. Finally he turned and whispered in my ear:

"The local psychiatrist is sitting right in the front row!" I looked, expecting from the concern the vicar was showing to see a Mephistophelian figure, perhaps with a little black goatee and thick-lensed spectacles! Instead I saw a very pleasant-faced little man, waiting in obvious expectancy for my address. Afterwards, the doctor was one of the first to come to me and introduce himself.

"Doctor N.," I said, "tell me—what did you think of what I had to say?"

The psychiatrist broke into a happy smile:

"Oh," he said, "I think it's wonderful to hear the tremendous things God is doing today!"

"What do you think of *me*?" I asked, knowing as a counsellor myself that he must have been sizing me up as I talked.

He pursed his lips and raised his eyebrows. "Well," he said, happily, "you remind me rather of the man who taught me psychiatry!"*

At the time that I was touring New Zealand telling of the work of the Spirit, two Anglican monks from a well-known order in England were also travelling through the country, conducting retreats. I encountered one of them quite early in my stay.

"I'm so glad to meet you, Father Bennett," he said. "You see, I believe in the Baptism in the Holy Spirit, and I want to receive it. I feel that I have a strong work of the Holy Spirit in my life, but I can't seem to speak in tongues!"

We talked awhile, and I tried to point out to him what might be inhibiting him from entering into full freedom in the Spirit. We prayed together, but he just couldn't seem to "let go." As we parted, he said, with a gentle smile:

"I'll just keep praying about it, Dennis!"

"That's wonderful, Father W.," I replied, "but don't forget to keep *trying*, too!"

I pointed out to him that speaking in tongues was something that *he* was going to do—that no amount of praying or seeking was going to help him very much until he could get up his nerve to open his mouth, and trust the Holy Spirit to give him words as *he* spoke.

"You've got to begin speaking and trust the Lord to do the guiding," I said.

It was as I completed my circuit of the country and was

* A number of believing psychologists and psychiatrists have received the Baptism in the Holy Spirit; also many members of these professions who are not Christians themselves tend to be friendly toward the Pentecost experience because of its stabilizing and integrating effect on the lives of people.

returning to Auckland by way of Hamilton that one of the priests I was with said:

"Did you know that Father W. is in Huntley? He's laid up with a bad back—can't get out of bed. He wants some of us to come and pray with him!"

Three of us made the short journey to the little town of Huntley. We were admitted to the vicarage, and to the bedroom where Father W. was. I could tell at once that there was something about him which was not quite the same.

"Hello, Dennis!" he said, "I'm glad to see you again. You know," he went on, "I'm beginning to speak in tongues! I do when I first wake up in the morning. I can't seem to keep going, but at least I start!"

There was a change in this man of God. The same quiet graciousness was there, but it was different. There was a freedom—a relaxed look about him that hadn't been there before he had begun to speak in tongues. We laid hands on him, prayed for him, and anointed him with oil in the Name of the Lord. Then we three ministers, we "men of faith," said our goodbyes and left the room to spend a few moments visiting with the vicar and his wife before going back to Hamilton. We were standing with our backs to the hall door. I remember that I had squatted down on the floor to talk with one of the younger members of the vicar's family, a little boy of some three years. Suddenly we were startled by a greeting from the hall:

"Hello in there!"

We looked round—it was Father W. He chuckled at our surprise.

"You prayed for me, and I got healed!" he said. "Didn't you expect me to?"

I returned to Auckland after nearly three weeks, and again

found myself in the home of the archdeacon for a last visit before leaving the country.

"I just can't tell you what's been going on since you left, Dennis," he said. "There has been a steady stream of people coming to our door—sick people, sad people, mixed up people. We have been praying for them, counselling them, even now and then asking deliverance for people who were obviously demon-possessed! We've been busy almost continuously—and we have seen results, too!"

The Holy Spirit had got them *involved*.

20

"Two by Two"

"Great Scott!" I clapped my hand to my forehead. "I've forgotten to bring my suits!" We were standing, Rita and I, in the baggage-claiming area of the Miami International Airport.

I had come back with a high heart, the ten thousand miles from New Zealand to Florida, to marry Rita. Three weeks spent on the other side of the world had brought home only the more clearly how much Rita had come to mean to me. All those long-distance calls reaching my fiancee at the strangest hours were most enjoyable, but not really satisfactory. (I never did get the time differential straight. Was it seven or eight hours? Was it yesterday or tomorrow?) But now we were together.

The wedding had been beautiful. All of Rita's immediate family had been there; even her mother, although she had been very weak and ill for some time, was given special strength. Her parents were actually the last guests to depart from the reception! My older son, stationed at a nearby Air Force Base, had served as best man, and his wife as bridesmaid. We'd been married October 15, 1966, in the little House of Prayer Episcopal Church in Tampa, and I had not thought of myself as a nervous bridegroom until this moment! We were on our way to Nassau, and my suits, except the one I was wearing, were hanging in their travelling bag in a closet in Tampa—with no reasonable way to secure them!

The informality of the Bahamas being what it is, this proved to be no great emergency after all. It was prophetic of our future together, that we returned to the mainland after just a few days to conclude our honeymoon at a conference on the work of the Holy Spirit at Ft. Lauderdale. And this has been our life ever since: telling people about Jesus, and about the full and wonderful life in His Holy Spirit.

"Hey, here's an invitation that looks interesting!"

I was opening the mail in the kitchen one afternoon shortly after our return to Seattle. Rita was standing at the stove stirring something that smelled very appetizing. It was good, after three years of fending for myself, to have good companionship —and good cooking! Rita put down her spoon.

"What is it?" she asked.

"The Full Gospel Business Men's Fellowship up in Calgary, Canada, wants me to come to some meetings. There's an invitation from the Anglicans, too; in fact, the Bishop himself has agreed to speak at the FGBMFI breakfast!"

"That sounds wonderful!" she responded, wiping her hands on her apron.

I looked at her. "Yes," I said, suddenly doubtful, "but you know something? I don't want to take off for Canada without you. I've been going places by myself for a long time, and I'm kind of tired of it."

I had never really enjoyed myself travelling alone, although it had been unavoidable in the past. Now with all the children grown and married, what was there to stop Rita from going with me? Besides, she had had an active ministry of her own before we were married. Did God intend her to give this up? Couldn't we share together in the work? I put these questions to Rita.

"It's a good idea," she said. "You know I'd love to go with you; but Dennis, that means travel fares for two—do you think it would be practical?" She hesitated a moment, then added: "Well, if the Lord wants it that way, He'll provide the funds, won't He?"

And He did just that. When one of our good friends heard of my invitation to Calgary, she said:

"Now you're not going up there without your bride!" and she gave us a good-sized cheque to go towards Rita's expenses.

This first journey settled the question, for we found that we were able to accomplish much more together than we could working separately. We were reminded that Jesus did send His disciples out "two by two." Rita could be talking to one group while I spoke to another. She could address a women's group while I was with the men. After I had given my testimony we could divide the meeting, and while I answered questions, Rita could immediately move into another room and begin to instruct through the Scripture those who were desiring to receive the Holy Spirit. The harvest of people receiving the Baptism in the Holy Spirit increased, and our own spiritual morale was higher than if we had not been together.

Due to our greater usefulness and effectiveness working together, the Lord was able to bless us more fully, and there was no financial problem; in fact, we finished further "in the black" than I had ever done when by myself! Since that first trip to Calgary, Rita and I have made most of the "missionary journeys" together.

In Calgary, I had just concluded my talk one evening in St.

Michael-and-All-Angels Anglican Church, and was answering questions. As always, there was much interest in "speaking in tongues." What is it? What does it mean? A woman raised her hand.

"Father Bennett," she said, "I have always thought of "speaking in tongues" as a very emotional and excitable experience, and I've always been afraid of it. You talk as though it wasn't like that at all, and as if you could speak in tongues at will any time you chose. Would you be willing to do that right here?"

The questioner was obviously very much in earnest. I said: "I'll speak 'in the Spirit' as we close the meeting; then I'll give a blessing in English." So, as I closed the meeting, I spoke briefly, accepting the words that came to my lips as guided by the Holy Spirit. As I began to speak, I felt a quickening of excitement, as though something unusual was about to happen. The language that came to my lips was different from any I had ever heard before, but as soon as I had concluded this prayer "in tongues" and had given a brief blessing, another hand was raised.

"But—but—" stammered a little lady sitting in the front row, "you surely know the language you were speaking, don't you?"

"No, I do not," I answered. "I have never heard it before."

"Why," she said, "that was Nepali!"

Nepali? I had to think for several minutes before realizing that this would of course be the language of Nepal, a country bordering Tibet on the south side of the Himalayas. The woman continued:

"My brother is a Jesuit missionary in Nepal. I am very fond of him, and I've been much concerned about his safety. It's a 'hot spot' for Christians, you know. He sent me a tape recording recently on which he read the Epistle for 'Gaudete'* Sunday, from the fourth chapter of Philippians, in the Nepali language. I have listened to it over and over, and you have just repeated it word for word!"

Faced with this major miracle of speech, this Roman Catholic woman received the Baptism with the Holy Spirit that night, and she too began to rejoice in a heavenly language far beyond the limitations of man's earthbound intellect. So, incidentally, did the woman who had first asked the question!

Rita and I didn't do much more long-distance travelling through the first year of our marriage. There was too much to keep us busy at home. I had been carrying on a multiple ministry ever since receiving the Holy Spirit in 1959, and especially since coming to St. Luke's. There was a continuous stream of people, including ministers and priests, coming to counsel with me. Also there was a fairly steady stream of visitors dropping in from just about everywhere imaginable to see what was going on. One of these, a Roman Catholic, a man whose business took him all over the world, said:

"I have heard of this church in London, England; Cape Town, South Africa; Buenos Aires, Mexico City, and Tokyo, and always from people in my own church! I had to come here to see what was happening!"

The normal work schedule of a minister in an average-size church is from sixty to seventy hours per week. I was ridicu-

---

* "Gaudete" Sunday means "Rejoice Sunday" and is the Roman Catholic name for what other liturgical churches would call the "Fourth Sunday in Advent." The name is taken from the first word of the Epistle: "Rejoice in the Lord alway: and again I say, rejoice. Let your moderation be known unto all men. The Lord is at hand. Be careful for nothing; but in every thing by prayer and supplication with thanksgiving let your requests be made known unto God. And the peace of God, which passeth all understanding, shall keep your hearts and minds through Christ Jesus." (Philippians 4:4–7)

lously busy, single-handedly trying to direct a large parish, while having many other demands. In fact, that year, my senior warden, a man skilled in personnel planning, said to me:

"Dennis, have you ever stopped to figure out how many hours you are trying to put in per week?"

"No, as a matter of fact, I haven't," I replied. "But I know that many times I feel frustrated in this never-ending job!"

He urged me to make a little survey, which showed that in order to accomplish the very minimum of what I wanted to do, I would have to put in two hundred and thirty hours weekly! There aren't even that number of hours *in* a week!

As for Rita, ever since coming to St. Luke's she had been receiving invitations to conduct Bible studies in Seattle and the surrounding cities. She had also found important work to do among the teen- and college-age people at the church. In addition to this, a radio ministry was opening for us. I had for several years given a half-hour radio talk each Sunday in Seattle. Now Rita and I together made this a question and answer programme which was so well received that it expanded to an hour. It was soon suggested that we should have the same type of programme in the Los Angeles area. After a trial period, an effective Christian radio station* offered us a half-hour slot five evenings a week on a noncommercial basis, which we accepted.

Invitations to speak continued to come, and I did not like to have to refuse so many of them, at home and abroad, because I knew how desperately the witness of the work of the Holy Spirit in the Church today was needed. Numerous ministers had shared with me the many concerns over their languishing churches. I also knew that doors which were opening might not be open indefinitely.

In the fall of 1967 God began to bring the answer. The Rev.

* KHOF-FM 99.5 mhz Glendale, Calif.

Richard Driscoll joined the staff of St. Luke's. I had known Father Dick and his wonderful family for several years, and now he felt led to come and be my associate. As soon as it was reasonable to do so after his arrival, I approached my vestry.

"Brethren," I said, "I want your backing in a decision. I've got to face the fact that I can't continue indefinitely trying to do three or four things at once. I don't want to leave St. Luke's, but I know that I must be free to carry on the outreach ministry God has given me, in good conscience—without feeling that I am neglecting one task to do another. You have always been very helpful and open-minded about this, because you know there's a big job to be done, but I am under a good deal of tension trying to be fair to all concerned. Now that I have a capable associate, I want you to approve a kind of semi-sabbatical year for me. Until June of next year I want to spend half of my time at St. Luke's, and the other half of my time travelling, speaking, writing, and generally carrying on an outreach ministry." My vestry concurred with this suggestion, not only without dissent, but without even a discussion!

Feeling a new freedom to do so, right after the first of the year I accepted an invitation to go to Jamaica. This came through an interdenominational group of Christians in Ft. Lauderdale, Florida, who had formed themselves into a "Committee of Forty" to sponsor conferences on the work of the Holy Spirit. Several of the members of this group had been going down to Montego Bay, proclaiming the good news of the full gospel. Already their ministry had resulted in the conversion of two of the leading communists in Jamaica! One of these, a woman of great talent, had been trained in several communist countries of Europe, and in Russia and China, for the proposed Communist take-over of the Caribbean. Now all of her ability and training was on the side of the Lord Jesus Christ!

For two nights I conducted meeting at St. James Anglican Church in Montego Bay, and then we left for the "back country."

We had been asked to spend a few days in St. Elizabeth's Parish in Southfield, a collection of some six Anglican congregations headed by a young English vicar and his wife. As we ministered to these people we noticed again that the hunger was the same, and the Lord's response to that hunger was the same! Nothing could be more diverse that the native Jamaican; there are strains of many nations and races mingled together in these people, but the effect of salvation through Jesus Christ and the Baptism in the Holy Spirit was exactly the same as in New York City, England, Alaska, or New Zealand. We were surprised at the freedom with which we were allowed to testify, not only in churches and church schools, but also in the public schools. At the Hampton School, a government-sponsored school for girls in Southfield, we talked to the whole student assembly. We told them what Jesus Christ had been doing in our lives, and in the lives of young people in the U.S. At the end of the meeting, we asked those who were interested in receiving Jesus Christ and being baptized in the Holy Spirit to stay behind. The entire student body stayed! Thinking that they did not understand what I was talking about, I tried to explain again that this was just for those who really meant business. Most of them still sat tight! Accordingly, we went round that auditorium and prayed with about seventy-five girls. Some needed to accept Christ as Saviour, and twenty-five of them were baptized in the Holy Spirit.

From the warmth of the Caribbean we found ourselves, several weeks later, heading to the far and frozen north! The Episcopal archdeacon of the Arctic had been interested in my ministry ever since my second visit to that largest state, and now wanted us to come to Kotzebue and Point Hope for a week in each place. Kotzebue is the largest Eskimo village in the area, and boasts all kinds of modern conveniences—seven stores and a fine electric power and lighting system. It's truly "downtown" by Arctic standards! Hunters come there from many places to stalk the polar bear, which is done nowadays, somewhat unfairly, by airplane! For me it was a renewal of acquaintances with some of the folk who had made me welcome in '64. We stayed at the home of the vicar and his wife and enjoyed it all thoroughly. Everything was new to Rita, since this was her first visit to Alaska: muktuk, caribou, seal— the only thing that stopped us was Eskimo ice-cream, a concoction of creamed seal-oil and fruit. We couldn't quite acquire the taste! The local people had an Eskimo dance in our honour, and we wondered at the amazing vigour of some of our older Eskimo friends in their seventies, entering into the symbolic and energetic dancing with the vitality of youth!

The most far-flung portion of our trip was Point Hope. This tiny Eskimo village is the farthest north and west you can go in the United States! It is located on a sand-spit projecting into the Chukchi Sea, about 150 miles north and east of Siberia! It is reached only by sea, by air, or by dog team! (Nowadays many Eskimo have gasoline-powered sleds which they use for short hauls, but it would be foolhardy to trust one's life on a long journey on one of these. The dog team is slower, but it is more reliable.) The ocean was frozen solid, we didn't have the time to go by dog sled, so we went by air. The Pilatus-Porter is an awkward-looking aircraft. Originally built to be powered with a reciprocating engine but later equipped with the much lighter turbine, which necessitated lengthening the nose, the plane looks much like a large praying mantis. Somehow the resemblance is heightened when the Porter takes off, lurching into the air at some ridiculously slow speed, after what seems to be only a few yards of take-off roll! It is, however, an intensely practical airplane for difficult conditions; it was built for mountain work in the Alps.

We climbed into the plane, together with the only other passenger, a pleasant-faced Eskimo lady, and the pilot. Baggage and freight were piled high behind us with no protecting barrier—it was evident that no one was counting on any sudden stops! We took off into beautiful clear air and began our hour-and-a-half flight. Mile upon mile of frozen, snow-covered tundra unrolled beneath us, broken only once by a tiny collection of houses between the mountains and the frozen shore.

"Kivalina," our pilot explained. Then he said:

"There's Point Hope!"

I looked ahead, and all I could see was a bank of low stratus clouds completely obscuring the site where the village lay. I waited for our captain to say: "We'll go back to Kotzebue and try again tomorrow!" but he didn't, he just flew on—over the top of the fog, around and around. The nose of our craft was cocked high in the air, our airspeed minimal. My own pilot's sensibilities told me that we were skirting a stall.

"Wonder what he's doing?" I whispered to Rita. She had done enough flying to be a little apprehensive of his manoeuvres.

"I don't know," she whispered back; "looks like we could stall any minute." Just then our pilot saw what he wanted—a break in the clouds below us that revealed, for a moment, the brief stretch of ice and snow that was the runway. Down through that rift we went like a shot partridge; down went all the flaps we had, which was plenty! The airplane shuddered and seemed to stop in mid air as we sank on to the runway. I fully believed that that pilot had his prop in reverse pitch before we were on the ground. What flying! Our skis touched the runway, and we slid about fifty yards and came to a gentle stop in front of what seemed to be the whole village. The arrival of what was hopefully called the "daily" airplane—it sometimes could not get in or out for as much as ten days at a time—was an event, and everyone was there to celebrate it, and to welcome the strangers from the South 48! The zero temperature and blowing fog encrusted everything in icy rime, but the human atmosphere was jovial. Our Eskimo travelling companion was welcomed into the bosom of her family, while Rita and I were whisked off by the Hannums to their cosy little house on the edge of the village, overlooking the frozen sea. It was hard to keep our footing as we walked over the little hills and valleys of snow covering the ground to a depth of many feet. My mukluks were made with uguruk skin, the hide of the big seal, and were actually intended for wet rather than dry snow; as we returned home from the meeting each evening, I always seemed to manage to fall and slide down the snowbank right outside the rectory!

Point Hope is a town of some four hundred Eskimo, and about eight Caucasians—three church leaders, and about five schoolteachers. The village lives by hunting and fishing, whaling being the big thing.

"Like to take a walk this morning?" Walter grinned at me across the breakfast table. I swallowed my last spoonful of cereal, wiped my mouth on my napkin, and said, "Sure! What's up?"

"Let's go over to the cemetery," Walter said. " 'Bout a half-mile over that way," he gestured. "Put on your parka, and muffle up good—you'll need it!"

He was right. When we went outside we found the temperature hovering a little above zero. Walter tucked his hunting rifle under his arm and we left the house.

"Might meet a bear or a wolf," he said encouragingly! A brisk breeze with a sprinkling of snow in it stung our faces as we stumped along over the drifts in the direction of what looked like bent sticks projecting from the snow about a half-mile to the north. As we got a little closer I saw that these curved sticks made a fence surrounding a rectangular area, with other sticklike objects, only much taller, standing on the inside.

"Whalebones," my guide explained. "They don't have any wood hereabouts, so this is what they use."

When we arrived at the little graveyard I saw that the grave markers were similarly fashioned—some of them eighteen feet and more high, the jawbones of gigantic whales inscribed with a cross, and the name of the person. Looking over the snowy tundra I saw another collection of huge whalebones, marking off a smaller area about a quarter of a mile from where we were standing.

"What are those?" I inquired.

"That's where one of the old chiefs is buried," the archdeacon explained. They claim he was a powerful witch doctor who gained great influence over the village nearly a hundred years ago. Among other evils, he encouraged the villagers to make distilled liquor. It's very dangerous to them in the wintertime. If a man gets a little drunk, he feels warm, and is likely to go out into the cold without proper protection. Many have been frozen to death in that way."

I nodded. "I saw the warning in the post office," I said.

"Yes. Well, they have to keep reminding folk about it. Anyway, the coast guard was finding so many frozen corpses that they actually appealed for a Christian missionary to be sent to the village. That's how the Episcopal Church comes to be here. The first missionary came about three-quarters of a century ago, and built the little church on the outskirts of the village. Today about eighty per cent of the population is Episcopalian."

Each afternoon, during most of our stay, we met in the church with the young people of the village. About thirty came

—all ages and sizes from ages nine or ten, to maturing young adults of eighteen and nineteen. We soon found ourselves not looking forward to this session, for the youngsters were restless after a long day at school, and not inclined to take us too seriously!

According to the tradition of the village, whenever a whaling captain finished the yearly re-covering of his boat with fresh sealskin, he was to treat all the children of the village to candy. At this time of the year, the only "candy" the small general store had was bubble gum, so one day the kids all showed up chewing massive quantities of gum and popping bubbles every so often! Knowing that she was going to be the victim the next day, Rita asked for help. In closing the meeting Archdeacon Hannum said:

"Tomorrow, please park your bubble gum on the snow outside before you come into the church!"

It helped a little, but as Rita told the story of how the Lord had worked in her own life when she was a young person, a number of the boys were squirming and giggling, although some of the girls were attentive. The general effect was still pretty unruly, and I was quite fed up with them. Just before the meeting ended Rita consulted with me:

"Dennis, I think we should invite those that want to, to come to the altar for a blessing." I felt she was thinking in terms of our experience with the young people in Jamaica, the month before. I failed to see the similarity. Those Jamaican kids had been well-behaved, courteous, and interested, but these seemed to be just the opposite. However, I couldn't very well say:

"I don't want to pray for God's blessing on them." But I certainly had my doubts as to whether it would "take"! I consented, rather unwillingly, to invite those who wanted to, to come forward, and dismissed the others. Almost the entire crew came forward and knelt at the altar rail, and around the choir stalls. Still, as they came, some dragged their feet and banged their heels, but as we began to pray with them, a new spirit of sincerity settled on them. Rita and Archdeacon Hannum were praying down one side of the chancel, while the Rev. Donald Oktollik was helping me. Donald, a much respected member of the community, had been the head of one of the two whaling lodges into which the village was divided; he had recently been ordained deacon, and was currently preparing for the priesthood. We asked each youngster whether he had accepted Jesus into his life. Most of them knew definitely that they had done this, but there were six or seven who had not. These we encouraged to receive the Lord, and as they did, one after another began to weep. The whole atmosphere became sweet with the presence of the Lord. The situation had changed so drastically, that after we had gone round once, we decided to go around again, and pray for them to be baptized in the Holy Spirit. This we did, and a very large percentage of those once-unruly children began to speak in other tongues!

The difference in the attitude of these teenagers was amazing! Whereas up to now they had been friendly enough, but in a "smart-aleck" kind of way, showing little respect, now they followed us around like little puppy dogs, wanting to go with us everywhere. As we were walking along over the snowdrifts down the middle of the village, one of a group of girls called to Rita:

"Mrs. Bennett, Mary is singing in the Spirit!" * Rita didn't

---

* St. Paul, in I Corinthians 14:15 refers to "singing with the spirit." This means allowing the Holy Spirit to inspire our spirit not only to speak, but to sing as He gives the words and the tune. Some who are unable to sing at all "in the natural," find that they can sing in the Spirit beautifully, if they trust the Holy Spirit to guide their voices. Sometimes during a prayer and praise time the entire group will join in "singing in the Spirit," allowing the Holy Spirit not only to guide individual voices, but to blend them and produce harmonies that sometimes sound like the angelic choir itself!

hear at first, because she was swallowed up in the big hood of the parka trying to keep her face protected from the blowing wind and snow, but when she finally understood she realized that this young girl, with no instruction from us—as we had not at this time mentioned the possibility—had begun to sing in the Spirit!

During our mission in Point Hope, the older generation met each morning for Bible study with Rita, with the Eskimo deacon, Donald Oktollik, as interpreter, and I spoke to a full church each evening. Having an interpreter also came in handy when praying with many of these older folk to receive the Baptism in the Holy Spirit. Donald helped us to determine whether they were speaking in Eskimo or in tongues! Donald, and his gentle wife, Lily, had both prayed to receive the Holy Spirit early in the beginnings of our meetings. Lily had "come through," but Donald, more inhibited, had not yet spoken in tongues. One evening though, as he helped us pray with some of his friends, forgetting his own self-consciousness in his eagerness to help the others, he too began to speak in the new language that God had for him!

It was so amazing to look at the happy faces of these dear people.

"Taiku!" they would say—the Eskimo version of our English "thank you"—or: "Kuyanak!" their own word. Then, in hesitant English: "This what we look for!" Many of these had met Jesus a long time before, but they knew there was more for them. Now they had it, and they knew it!

At the closing church service in Point Hope, as I looked out at the faces of these good friends in Jesus, I could not miss the fact that in spite of ethnic and cultural differences, these faces looked just like the faces of the Seattle-ites who had been baptized in the Holy Spirit. The same open happy shine was there, the same joy in their eyes. The same Spirit of grace was working in them. It was impossible to miss the literal truth of the Gospel that when we accept Jesus we are born again into a new family, and all become brothers and sisters in the Spirit. "You shall be witnesses of Me, after that the Holy Ghost has come upon you . . ." means far more than witnesses in speech alone.

Our other long journey in 1968 was a return to England. As before, it was the Rev. Michael Harper and the Fountain Trust who sponsored the tour, and we visited London, Bournemouth, Bristol, Birmingham, Liverpool, Teesside, Hull, Normanton, Bradford, Coventry, and many other places. Again we visited many schools and churches, mostly, but by no means all, Anglican. I spoke at Birmingham Cathedral and had many fruitful contacts with the clergy and bishops of the Church of England. We had opportunity to see how effectively the charismatic renewal is continuing to move forward in the British Isles.

At an Anglican Church near London, a woman came forward for healing prayer. She had had arthritis in both knees for many years, and was in much pain. We will not forget how she literally jumped for joy when the Lord Jesus, through prayer and the laying on of hands, took away the pain and crippling, and she was able to walk normally!

We had long been admirers of the rugged saint of the Pentecostal movement, Smith Wigglesworth. What delight to find ourselves in his hometown of Bradford, Yorks! Here we conducted an evening meeting, and when it ended, I remained in the auditorium with those who had theological questions to ask, while Rita retired to an adjoining room to instruct fifty people who wished to receive the Holy Spirit. As a teenage girl started to speak in the Spirit, in a language unknown to her, a young woman nearby expressed great surprise.

"Why," she exclaimed, "that girl is speaking perfect

French! And I should know, for I *teach* French in a local high school!"

We also attended an interesting conference at High Leigh, but perhaps the high point in the tour was the conference held in London at the very heart of the Church of England, "Church House," right next-door to Westminster Abbey! It was here, in the very auditorium we occupied, that one month later the bishops of the Anglican Communion from all over the world would meet for the Lambeth Conference. Indeed, I remarked to Rita:

"The speaker's chair which I sat in this evening is the very same one that the Archbishop of Canterbury will occupy next month as he presides at this worldwide conference!" On both nights of our charismatic conference many received Jesus into their lives, and on the second night seventy people received the Holy Spirit simultaneously, and all together began to speak "in new languages as the Spirit gave the utterance"!

21
A New Thrust

Before returning home from England, we spent a few days in Germany. I had been invited to take part in a conference of Roman Catholics, Lutherans, Reformed, Baptists, Orthodox, Anglicans, and others, all of whom had two things in common —a new freedom in the Holy Spirit, and the manifestation of His charismatic gifts. As a result, these leaders from various denominations were seeing God's love and power beginning to revive churches and communities. That conference brought me two new experiences: it was my first time of witnessing in a non-English-speaking country, and in a language other than English. I gave my testimony in German, a language with which I had some familiarity. One picture which remains indelibly fixed in my memory from this *Oekumenische Dienst* is the figure of "Bruder E.," a vigorous and scholarly Franciscan friar, who had just begun to "speak in tongues." This sturdy follower of the blessed Francis of Assisi, who himself spoke in tongues and whose followers were originally known for their childlike faith, was rather offended at the simplicity of his new experience, and declaimed with emphasis as we discussed the whole matter in his room one evening:

"Dies ist die Demütigkeit von meinem Intellekt!" (This is the humiliation of my intellect!)

We spent two refreshing days with the Mary-Sisters, the *Marienschwesternschaft* in Darmstadt. This Lutheran religious community for women began in the closing days of World War II, when Allied bombers were totally destroying city after city as Hitler's fall became imminent. A group of young women had been meeting for Bible study. Many of them had lost husbands and sweethearts in the tragedy of the war, and when one night they saw their home city transformed in a few hours into a smoking ruin, they determined to band together in a monastic life. The leaders took the names Mother Basileia and Mother Martyria and thus was launched a most amazing work of the Lord. With little worldly goods or support, but with tremendous faith in God and in the power of prayer, the community, in the face of almost impossible odds, established a retreat-centre and convent on a fifty-acre tract of land in the heart of the city of Darmstadt, which they christened *Kanaan-Land*. The first buildings were constructed with their own hands. They had no water, so they prayed for it, and now have fifty times as much as their neighbours!

Today the community includes a well-operated farm, an elaborately equipped printing shop, much beautiful landscaping, and many buildings, including a magnificent chapel. Many acts of charity and service are being performed by these women, not the least of which is the providing of a place of refreshment and retreat for any who wish to go there, without charge. A guest at the Mary-Sisters retreat houses only contributes anonymously as he feels led. One of their specific outreach works is with young people. When Dave Wilkerson *

---

* Dave Wilkerson is the young minister internationally known for work with New York gangs, set forth so admirably in the book, *The Cross and the Switchblade* (Bernard Geis Associates, 1962—Pyramid Books, 1964).

was in Darmstadt, he spoke and ministered to a crowd of several thousand teenagers in their church, while the sisters assisted in counselling the youngsters afterwards.

A most interesting thing about the Mary-Sisters is that shortly after their order was formed, they experienced a Pentecostal outpouring, with the manifestations of speaking in tongues, interpretation, prophesy, etc. This was almost unheard of among non-Pentecostals in the late forties, and they were not made popular by their experience! They "stuck to their guns" however, and today the Gifts of the Holy Spirit are a firmly established part of the devotional life of the community. Rita and I had the privilege of being invited to the private "prayer and praise" meeting of the sisters. We sat on the platform in the prayer chapel, with the superiors, the Lutheran chaplain of the order, and his wife, and listened and shared as the sisters sang folk-type choruses. Many of their songs were originals, given by the Holy Spirit during these meetings. Looking at the bright-faced women, most of them quite young, in their beige-and-white habits, raising their hands in praise, sometimes waving banners they had made with Scripture texts on them (they are strong on banners of all kinds!)—or at one point in the service, waving leafy branches in time to the music as they sang "in the Spirit"—we were again struck by the strangeness, and yet the familiarity of the scene. Eight thousand miles from home, in a foreign city and country, among people of another language and culture, behind the walls of a convent, we saw the Lord, the Holy Spirit, unfailingly at work in God's people. We knew that these girls would be instantly at home in a meeting at St. Luke's, Seattle. More than that, we knew that if we could have gathered together in one place these sisters, the friends who had received the Holy Spirit in Alaska, in Jamaica, in England, and in numerous different far-flung parts of the U.S.A., they would have required no introduction or explanation, but would have immediately been able to enjoy such a meeting as this together. I began to see more clearly what the Apostles' Creed means by the "Communion of Saints."

Arriving home, I found it hard to imagine that just a year before I had thought things were slowing down, or reaching a plateau!

"We seem to be coming to a saturation point," I had remarked to my wife. "During these last eight years, we've probably reached most of the people in Seattle who are interested." How wrong we were! Under Father Driscoll's capable leadership, the church had been booming in my absence; not only that, but it was evident that if my semisabbatical was to continue, Father Dick was going to have to have more help. He was beginning to get the same harried look that I had when he arrived to lift the load off my shoulders! We talked about it to the vestry, and they agreed to provide the salary to retain the services of another man, if we could find the right one. It wasn't long before my associate called me to tell me that a friend of his was interested in joining our staff, and after a brief time of getting acquainted, I formally invited the Rev. Thomas Bigelow to become my second associate. Several weeks after he had arrived and settled in, I listened to him telling his story at the Friday night meeting. To my great surprise, I found that I played a part in the story of his receiving the Holy Spirit! Then I remembered: we had prayed with this young man in our home in Van Nuys nearly nine years ago! At that time he was in business—although he had spent two years in seminary—but he had later gone back to complete seminary training, and had gone into the ministry.

With adequate leadership the parish began to grow even more rapidly. It became almost an embarrassment to discuss the state of the Church with other clergy, for their usual talk was one of woe—of shrinking budgets, shrinking church attendance, diminishing interest, loss of confidence, ministers leaving the ministry to enter lay professions—while all we could say about the condition of the Church was "Praise the Lord! God is moving, drawing many people, and changing lives!" So much did things continue to flourish that six months later we found ourselves retaining the services of a fourth man, a newly graduated seminarian, the Rev. Daniel Stewart. This kind of leadership set me free to do more speaking, writing, travelling, and general outreach and missionary activity, both at home and abroad.

Pentecostal Catholics

We were on a United Super DC-8 jet returning home from the east coast. For the first two hours of our flight we had been over an unbroken deck of clouds, but now I could see the stratus layers beginning to break apart, and glimpses of the ground beneath. I studied the map.

"Hm-m-m!" I said. "According to my navigation, we should be somewhere off the tip of Lake Michigan." The words had hardly left my mouth before our airplane flew into clear sky, and sure enough, there was Lake Michigan in the distance, sparkling and beautiful in the mid-afternoon sun, while just below us was a good-sized city.

"South Bend!" I hazarded. "It's too far from the lake to be Gary!"

Rita didn't pay too much attention to my navigational exploits, but she murmured, half to herself: "South Bend—oh, that's where Notre Dame University is! Just think, Dennis, they're going to have another conference there this year for 'Catholic Pentecostals' as they call themselves. They had around six hundred in attendance last year, and they expect more than a thousand this time."

I nodded. "That's great, isn't it?" As I leaned back into my seat, my thoughts flew on ahead of our airplane. I saw again the recent meeting in Missoula, Montana, when I addressed seven hundred people before the high altar of St. Anthony's Catholic Church, and later prayed with some forty-five who remained to receive the Baptism in the Holy Spirit.

In retrospect I realized that in all my years of being in the ministry I had had almost no contact with the Roman Catholic Church; in fact, I had been more than a little afraid of Roman Catholic clergy! Then one morning the vicar of our Episcopal Mission in a small town in eastern Washington took me to breakfast with the Roman Catholic rector and his assistant. He listened very carefully, and then put up a careful theological fence. When he saw that I had no intention of knocking it down, he said:

"Actually, there's nothing in this that is contrary to the teachings of the Catholic Church!"

I was surprised at his openness, but did not think much more about it until a year or two later. I was in Boston for a series of meetings, and returned very late one night to the home of the man who was co-ordinating my schedule to find three people waiting to see me: one was a pleasant-faced young man in a clerical collar, the other two, from their happy looks, and from the "Praise the Lord!" with which I was greeted, I took to be members of my friend's Assembly of God Church. It turned out that the first young man was a Roman Catholic priest who was eagerly seeking the Baptism in the Holy Spirit, and the two laymen, also Roman Catholic, had both already received the Holy Spirit. We had a good visit far into the wee, small hours of the morning, and I began to get an inkling of how the walls were crumbling.

Then came a full-scale encounter. It was in England in 1965.

Thanks to that wonderful servant of God, David DuPlessis,* whom God had used to open doors in many unexpected places to the witness of the Baptism in the Holy Spirit, I had been invited to speak to the Jesuit Training College at Chipping Norton, near Oxford. It was with some trepidation that I entered upon this assignment. I shall not soon forget our entrance into that huge building that night, with its echoing corridors, and massive and forbidding appearance. But as soon as we (Michael Harper was with me) were met at the door, we were enveloped in warmth and love, and felt immediately at home. Our hosts were the Principal of the College, the Rev. Father Murray, S.J., and the well-known Jesuit scholar and Oxford don, the Rev. Dr. Bernard Leeming, S.J. That night, as I faced some hundred or more young men, my trepidation returned. Of these fellows, a good proportion had degrees in philosophy from Oxford or Cambridge, and they were going on to intensive graduate study. What was I to say to them? I knew I didn't want to cross scholarly swords with them! The answer was simple enough—I told them my story: told them how I had accepted the Lord Jesus, and how I had been baptized in the Holy Spirit. In no way was I challenged. A great proportion of those young men stayed for an hour afterward, and asked me all the same questions that young Methodists, or young Episcopalians, ask. Their interest was deep and genuine, and they had no quarrel, it seemed, with my theology! Even after that, a dozen of them stayed on to talk over tea, and then the Principal and I talked on far into the night.

I had a foretaste through these experiences of what perhaps is currently the most unexpected aspect of this charismatic renewal, and that is the great and deep interest and participation on the part of the Roman Catholics. In 1967 we were all

---

* *The Spirit Bade Me Go*, by David DuPlessis, distributed by Logos International, Plainfield, N.J.

surprised to hear of a strong movement of the Holy Spirit at Notre Dame University. That story has been well told in Kevin and Dorothy Ranaghan's book *Catholic Pentecostals*. Later, I was asked to speak to a group of the theological faculty and students at Gonzaga University in Spokane, and was again pleased at the acceptance I received, not only of my person and my testimony, but of my doctrine. A young Jesuit member of the faculty came up to me at the end of my talk and said:

"Father Bennett, I have just completed a book on the Holy Spirit, and I want you to know that I agree with everything you have said here today!"

My thoughts were re-called to the present by a few quivers of turbulence, and glancing up, saw that our captain had lighted the "Fasten Seat Belt" warning. I dutifully tightened my belt, and returned to my thoughts.

Early in 1968 we had met Father Fulton, the rector of one of the largest Roman Catholic churches in our part of Seattle. He had become acquainted with Ron, a young man from St. Luke's who had been marvellously healed by Jesus Christ, both physically and psychologically. Ron and his wife Sally invited us to dinner to meet their friend. We had found Father Fulton to be a kindly and humble person who certainly knew and loved the Lord Jesus. In fact it was he who suggested that we each tell how we met Christ. He heard with great interest our experience of the Holy Spirit and His gifts, but that was as far as the matter went at that time. Then, a month or two later, I received a call from Father Fulton.

"Dennis," he said, "can you come over to St. Thomas Seminary tomorrow? We are having a series of lectures on communications and preaching, and the instructor is a young man from the Midwest, Father McNutt. He is a Dominican monk, and claims to have this same experience that you have, the

Baptism in the Holy Spirit. He speaks in tongues! And he wants to meet you—can you come over?"

You bet I could! At the seminary the next day I met Father McNutt and found he had been praying with some of the local clergy, and that several of them had already received the Holy Spirit. After lunch a few priests joined Father McNutt and myself for further discussion.

"I'm so depressed," one of them said. "I've got to find something to help me, or I don't know what I'm going to do." As I looked at the distressed face of the young priest who had spoken, I was reminded of the priest of my own denomination at the clergy conference eight years before who had received the Holy Spirit along with the first St. Lukan's. Was history about to repeat itself? We prayed with him, and as he began to speak in tongues we saw the miracle happen again. His countenance cleared—he relaxed visibly as he lifted his voice to God in words unknown to him, words given by the Holy Spirit. At the same time, something else was happening. Father Fulton, the man who had invited me to visit the seminary that day, had been sitting back in a corner listening to all that was going on, and he, too, quietly began to speak in tongues!

Then the doors seemed to fly open. The next night I was invited to a prayer meeting with twenty Roman Catholic priests. Since that night they have been meeting weekly! It became not at all unusual to have twelve or so Roman Catholic sisters sitting in our prayer meeting at St. Luke's, often with their hands upraised in prayer and praise. Rita and I began to be asked to address convents in Seattle, Tacoma, and Spokane, and these invitations have continued to come. On our last journey to the eastern part of the country, we were asked to stop off in Odessa, Texas, to conduct a two-day mission at a Roman Catholic Church. We spent a wonderful time ministering to a basically Mexican-American congregation, where both the priests and the parish worker are Catholic Pentecostals, together with an increasing number of the congregation. In our two days at this church, nothing was said or done that would have seemed strange to any other "Full Gospel" group of Christians. The literature displayed on the book tables was derived largely from evangelical and Pentecostal sources. Again we saw the Holy Spirit breaking down the walls of denominationalism, and bringing Christians into unity of heart.

On a trip to Berkeley, California, early in 1970, in one interdenominational meeting alone five Roman Catholic priests received the Baptism in the Holy Spirit. It seems that the late Pope John's prayer that Roman Catholics would experience a new Pentecost is being vividly answered!

My reverie was broken as the young man in the seat ahead of me stood up. He was tall—well over six feet—and very thin. His blond hair, rather obviously unwashed, reached to his shoulders. He was wearing a grimy buckskin shirt and faded jeans. As he turned toward me, my glance travelled upward, from the peace cross that hung from the string of beads around his neck, to his face. It was an intelligent-looking face, although mostly concealed by the scraggly and unkempt growth of beard, and by ridiculously oversized blue spectacles. Slung across one shoulder was a small guitar which the stewardess had vainly tried to persuade him to leave in the coat compartment. The general effect was climaxed by a wide-brimmed black hat. I recalled a comment I had recently heard: "Hippies are lost sheep masquerading as shepherds!" As my hippie neighbour disappeared down the block-long aisle of the airplane, I looked at Rita.

"Look familiar?" I asked.

She smiled, and bobbed her head. "Uh-huh. Reminds me of home on Friday night!"

By now at St. Luke's we were thoroughly accustomed to the hippie type. Our city had been having a serious time with drug use among young people, and our U district was replete with the kind of long-haired youth we had just seen; but a wonderful thing was happening. These lost sheep were beginning to turn to Jesus for some real answers.

It is strange now to look back at *with Youth* the youth group during my first weeks at St. Luke's. On that first Sunday night in July 1960 I discovered they were having a rock and roll dance in the church basement with the lights turned off! Typically, the patient people who were sponsoring the group had given up trying to do any more than entertain the kids and keep them out of mischief as much as possible, or at least trying to keep the mischief where it could be somewhat controlled! The picture began to change when some of the young people received the Holy Spirit along with their parents.

One night a leading layman in the church sought me out.

"Father Bennett, something terrible has happened!"

"What's bothering you, Wally?"

"Oh, those daughters of mine! You know both of them have been baptized in the Holy Spirit. Well, last night they got their neighbour friend over in the basement, and told her about their experience, laid hands on her, and she received the Holy Spirit!"

I roared with laughter! I couldn't help it, for the news was so far from being terrible! But Wally's expression remained very solemn.

"You don't understand, Father B.," he said. "Their dad is very much upset about all that is going on in the church!"

"Well," I said, "we can't expect the young people *not* to tell their friends about something as exciting as the Good News that Jesus is alive and real. Cheer up! It'll come out all right." And it did!

As time went by, more of the teenagers received the Holy Spirit, some through their parents' prayers, and some by talking and praying with one another. We soon had a sizable group of young people. It was great to see them taking part in the prayer meetings along with older people—for the Holy Spirit ignores differences in age, too.

As more and more adults came into the fellowship in the Holy Spirit, however, the younger people began to pull away into their own group again, and to our frustration we found ourselves once more confronted with the "youth group" problem—what to do with them, how to keep them "fired up," how to help them defend themselves in the mounting temptations of modern school life. In 1962 the Full Gospel Business Men had an international convention at Seattle with some very effective youth meetings. A lot more of our kids received the Lord and the Baptism in the Holy Spirit, and those who were already "with it" were revived and strengthened. That summer there was real freedom and joy among them.

"Just wait," they said, "till school starts! We'll really take over those ol' high schools for Jesus!" But alas, when school started and our young spiritual Don Quixotes mounted their chargers, all that ensued was a sickening thud! They found themselves not strong or effective enough to cope with the unbelief and evil they met, and whereas they did not desert their own faith, they did not move ahead with a victorious witness in their schools. Through the next few years the adults continued to move ahead, but the youth work rather languished. It had become a "line-holding" operation. In 1965 and '66 things began to pull together under the direction of a capable young couple, Jack and Sybil, and early in 1967 there began to be real freedom again. About this time our youth leaders asked my wife, Rita, to work with them and to help the young people learn how to enter into free worship and praise, expecting the gifts of the Spirit to be seen in their meetings. As they allowed the Holy Spirit to minister through them, they began to experience healings and miracles, to share exciting testimonies of what God was doing in their lives, of answered prayer and daily guidance. Many teenagers began to receive salvation and the Baptism in the Holy Spirit, and told their friends at school.

"What's happened to you? You look so darn happy!"

"Oh, I was at a prayer meeting last night. I found out how real God is, and asked Jesus to run my life from now on. Boy, do I feel good!"

"You what?"

"I accepted Jesus. Got healed, too. I had a bad cold, and the symptoms just disappeared when I was prayed for!"

"Wha-a-a-t? Well, if you've got anything like that, I want it, 'cause I'm messed up, man! Where do you go to church anyway?"

"St. Luke's Episcopal. But don't worry, you don't have to be an Episcopalian! No one will try to get you to join our church; they couldn't care less about what church you belong to. The important thing is for you to meet God!"

It wasn't long before the little meeting room under the church was crowded with teenagers the way it had been with adults before we built the new parish hall.

"Dennis," Rita said one evening as we were riding along in the car, "we need to have a meeting on Friday night for the teens like the one you have for adults. We need a meeting just for testimony, and to pray with kids to receive the Holy Spirit. Sunday night needs to be a 'believer's meeting' where the young people can be free to pray and praise the Lord, and to get into some good Bible study. If there are too many newcomers it kind of stiffens things up!"

"Fine with me," I said. "Why don't you youth sponsors talk it over, and come up with a plan."

They did, and before long we started to have as many as two hundred young people in the church basement in addition to the crowd of adults in the parish hall. Two more workers, John and Denny, came to fill in for the other youth leaders as duties called them elsewhere. Then, one night, for a special speaker, we rented the Rainier Room at the Seattle Centre to accommodate over eight hundred teenagers for our Friday night meeting!

I glanced out of the window, and saw the patchwork of the Mid West countryside rolling away beneath us. Rita had her eyes closed and seemed to be catching "forty winks." The Lord had certainly used her with the young people.

One high school in particular began to be greatly influenced by this move of God. In this one school alone, fifty kids had been baptized in the Holy Spirit. School teachers were saying:

"What's come over these young people? Virtue is stalking the halls unchecked!" Pretty soon many of these youngsters began to meet together every morning before class to pray for their school, among other things. It wasn't long before answers to prayer became evident. From time to time in the course of the last ten years, our young people have formed singing groups, and have gone out to reach others through music. Now a college-age group calling themselves the "New Men" had formed, and had been having real success in witnessing to young people by singing modern-style Gospel music, interspersed with their own testimonies of what Jesus has done for them. In '68 this group asked the principal of the aforementioned high school if they could sing for an assembly. He listened to them as they auditioned for him privately and said: "Yes. I think our students would enjoy hearing you, but there's one thing that I'll have to ask you to refrain from doing; you can't talk about church!"

"Oh, no sir," responded the leader of the group, with a grin.

"We wouldn't want to talk about church—that could be dull! But we would like to talk about Jesus. Is that okay?"

"Hm-m-m!" the principal said, no doubt thinking about Supreme Court decisions . . . "That's all right. He certainly was a good man: you can talk about Him."

For one solid hour this group held two thousand high-school kids spellbound as they played and sang, and told how Jesus had delivered them from drugs, from hopelessness and emptiness. At the end of the programme there was a standing ovation. The teachers said:

"We haven't had a standing ovation for an assembly programme for ten years!" The principal told the New Men:

"I'd like to see you get into every high school in Seattle!"

To date they have performed in nearly one-hundred high schools not only in Seattle but in other cities, with similar results. A second group, calling themselves the 'Fishers of Men' have now formed, and are having a fine ministry, more especially to church groups. It's good to know that similar work is going on, not only in the North West, but all over the country, and that through these ministries tens of thousands of young people are accepting Jesus Christ and being empowered by the Holy Spirit.

Every Friday night for the past three years, from seventy-five to two hundred teenagers gather at our church for a time of singing and inspiring testimonies—paralleling the meeting for adults—and every Saturday night some one hundred or more college-age youth meet to spend several hours in the same way. Some of the young adults still keep their uniform of long hair and strange, old-fashioned dress in order to "catch" others of their friends who need the same deliverance they have experienced.

I thought again about a Saturday night two years before, when this group was still meeting at our house. We had crowded over a hundred young people into our front and dining rooms, by dint of sitting them on the floor, so that we had "wall-to-wall people"! Out in the kitchen were ten or twelve "hip" kids who had come to see what was going on. They would not come into the main meeting, but watched and listened through the doorway, as one after another of the group told how Jesus had rescued them from drugs, or met other needs in their lives.

"I got into my father's liquor closet when I was just a little kid," said one young man. A good-looking, blond-haired fellow with a little moustache, he had kept a "semi-hippie" look, explaining, "If I look too 'straight,' the kids with problems won't come around, so I leave my hair a little long, and keep the gold-rimmed spectacles.

"I was soon on my way to becoming an alcoholic. Then as I got older I tried drugs—pot, LSD, and then speed. That speed is bad stuff. It caused my heart to beat so fast that I finally wound up with a heart attack, but that didn't stop me from taking some more. I was a mean one, too. I wanted to smash and blow things up! Then Jesus got hold of me! Wow, what a wonderful change! What a wonderful life! Now I want to live for God, and help people!" The young man's face was glowing as he told his story.

Pretty soon, the whole group broke into spontaneous praise. Someone started a chorus, and soon they were happily clapping and singing. The general feeling was that of a jolly party, and yet one knew that there was much more to it than that. God's presence and love was felt in that room, and the kids responded to it. One of the hippies turned to his friend standing near him in the kitchen.

"Hey, man, it's a good trip," he said eagerly, "it's a *good* trip!"

The ministry to the youth goes beyond just having meetings

at the church. Faced with the deadly challenge of drugs and psychedelic philosophy attempting to destroy the younger generation, a young couple who joined our congregation had felt directed by God to sell their business and rent a home in the university district just a few blocks away from the "Avenue" where the centre of the drug involvement was to be found. They then took in up to twenty-five drug addicts, young people who were willing to turn their lives over to Jesus, and attempt to break Satan's bondage. This work was all done strictly by faith—no appeals for funds at all. They carried on this work for about two years. St. Luke's people support them, pray for them, help them, but in no way sponsor them or try to tell them what to do—the Lord does that! In 1970 they closed the House of Zacchaeus and opened Zacc's Place, a coffeehouse in the basement of one of the nearby churches in the U district. Many chapters could be written about the exciting and productive ministry that they have been carrying out among needy young people.

One night two of the girls from the House of Z. were crossing the Montlake Bridge, when they saw a young boy about to throw himself into the canal. They dragged him to safety and literally sat on him until help could arrive! One of the girls said:

"It's lucky we were bigger than him!" John, the director of the house, arrived with reinforcements, and they took the youngster by main force to the House of Zacchaeus. All the way there he screamed and kicked and struggled, crying out that "God" had told him to jump off the bridge! At the home, John and his wife Diana tried to get the boy to listen to reason, but he still fought. At one point he broke away, rushed up the stairs, and was halfway out the window before he could be stopped.

John could see that the youngster needed prayer for deliverance, so he proceeded to cast out the spirit of suicide, in the

Name of Jesus. The boy calmed down immediately. Then John said:

"In thirty seconds, son, if you wish it to be so, you can be through with all this fear and darkness, and be filled with joy and happiness! All you have to do is ask Jesus to rescue you from all your misery, and come into your heart!"

He did just that. Jesus came into his life, and hell went out. Two weeks later John said:

"He's still smiling. Hasn't stopped since that first night!"

They discovered that the boy was from California, and had virtually been kidnapped by a drug-pushing gang and brought to Seattle. Shortly after this our friends had the great satisfaction of putting the young man on the bus and sending him home to his parents. They have since this time received good letters from him.

Again, like the other wonderful things that are happening, this new life among young people is worldwide in scope. In Palmerston North, New Zealand, the entire family of the treasurer of the local Anglican Parish had received the Holy Spirit. One of their children, a young boy, age nine, entirely on his own initiative started a prayer and praise session among his elementary schoolmates. Every morning before school, some twenty-five of them met at the school for this purpose. There was no adult leadership, and the teachers were especially impressed because the youngsters would come down to have their meeting even though it was a school holiday!

Another interesting encounter concerning youth took place in Christchurch, New Zealand. I had given my testimony that night in the little Anglican Church in Aranui. After the meeting a woman came up to me somewhat agitated.

"Mr. Bennett! I just want to say that I'm worried about my daughter. She's become involved with this movement you're talking about. It just isn't normal! She stays out until eleven o'clock going to these prayer meetings!"

"How old is your daughter?" I inquired.

"She's twenty."

"Hm-m. At twenty she could probably be trusted out till eleven o'clock, even at a prayer meeting!" I commented.

The woman nodded. "Yes, of course," she said, "but she doesn't go to parties, or dances, or anything—well, *normal*. It just isn't *normal* to be going to these religious things all the time!"

I didn't say anything. After a brief pause, my new acquaintance continued:

"Of course, she's really a very nice girl!"

"I'm sure she is," I agreed.

"And," said the mother a little more thoughtfully, "her brother goes out and stays very late, and sometimes comes home drunk." After a pause she added, laughing a little: "I guess I like the way she is acting better than the way he is!"

Then in England, in several widely separated places we found parish churches literally teeming with young people who had received the Lord Jesus and been baptized in the Holy Spirit. Many were children of agnostic or atheistic parents, some of whom were very worried about their "way-out" offspring! It was quite a switch to see teenagers meeting at church before the main meeting specifically for the purpose of praying for the conversion of their parents!

"You know," I said to Rita, "if I had been told ten years ago of all that is happening today, I would not have believed it *at all*!"

"These last ten years have been amazing for me too," replied Rita. "I want everyone to know how wonderful this life in the Spirit is!"

The soft drone of the jets was restful, and I was sleepy. The next thing I knew I was awakened by a sudden change of sound. Our pilot had reduced power for our descent as we emerged from the mountains to swing out over the coastal plain to the Seattle area. The last part of a jet flight is always fascinating to me, when the engines are cut back to a whisper, and the great bird is gliding along, seemingly without effort. The first twinkling lights were appearing throughout the city as we crossed Lake Washington. The traffic was jammed on the floating bridges and the freeways far below us. Up came the starboard wing as we turned "final." I looked across at the western sky. The sun was setting behind the snow-clad Olympics, throwing them into full relief.

My mind flashed to Indonesia, where what may well be the greatest spiritual breakthrough of our time has been taking place for several years now. I thought of the amazing manifestations of New Testament power being experienced there— the well-documented stories, carried by impartial observers, of people being raised from the dead, of thousands healed, and of even more startling miracles: walking on water, water being turned into wine, as God's people, very often humble and uneducated, see fulfilled the Biblical promise: "He that believes on me, the works that I do shall he do also; and greater works than these shall he do . . ."[1] I remembered hearing of the thousands of Mohammedans and Communists being won to Jesus Christ. Tired of killing one another, and disillusioned with the unsatisfactory answers of both of their religions, many are coming to Jesus and finding Him to be the answer. A missionary friend recently returned from Indonesia said to me:

"I tramped seventy miles into the interior—it was seventy miles to get a glimpse of heaven, as I heard these ex-Communists and ex-Mohammedans singing all day long the praises of the true God for the joy He has brought them." This same man, the head of a strong interdenominational missionary fellowship said also:

"I was a missionary to Indonesia many years ago. We would work for a year to get one convert from Mohammedanism to Christ, and then half the time he would recant. Now the Christians who used to be Mohammedans are organizing evangelistic teams to go to Pakistan to win other Mohammedans to Christ! It is incredible!"

My mind travelled on to South America from where reports come continually, telling of thousands upon thousands who are coming to know Jesus Christ. One leading evangelist—not himself a part of the charismatic movement—pointed out that some eighty per cent of the Christians in South America have the Pentecostal experience.

The flaps whined into full position, and the airframe shuddered as the pilot lowered the landing gear. As I looked to the east, windows caught the red glare of the western sky, as if many little fires were blazing. "Will there be blazes of riot and destruction in the coming years?" I asked myself. "Or fires of the Holy Spirit?" I looked at the city stretched out below, and realized the very small impact that had been made on this mass of humanity. I thought of the tensions, and the sorrows, the spiritual sickness, the hatred, the lostness, the misery spread out there.

We were nearly down now, and in a few moments I felt the familiar bump and squeal of the tyres on macadam, and then the roar of reversed engines. As we slowed and turned off the active runway on to the blue-lighted taxiway, I remembered the invitations and letters on my desk at home, from Sweden, Australia, India, Korea, Africa. So many other cities like this one, so many millions of people. I knew it would not be very long before we would be taking off again from this very runway. I thought of the many new opportunities for outreach that were opening, and the great need to tell of the power of Jesus Christ to change lives—filling them with His love—the need at home and abroad. I thanked God that the Holy Spirit is raising up more and more men and women everywhere to share in this vast work—the only eternally important work—that of telling the world that God is real, and God is available.

22
Acts Twenty-eight

The book of the Acts of the Apostles in the Bible, which could just as well be called the "Acts of the Holy Spirit," has no conclusion. So it is in writing about any follower of Jesus, or any group of His people: we can never find a stopping place. The last chapter of this book, too, like Acts 28, must finish open-ended. I wish I could tell all the things that have happened, and are happening, to the people who have appeared in the pages of this book, but that would be impossible. We can only take a quick glance at one group of Christians after a decade of teaching openly and experiencing freely the blessings of Pentecost.

Most of the Book of the Acts is about the Apostle Paul, and in the last chapter he is still going strong! He has in no sense "cooled off," or settled down! In Acts 28 we are told how, after being shipwrecked, Paul and his shipmates are on the island of Melita. In the process of gathering wood for the fire, Paul picks up a venomous snake and is bitten; but instead of falling down dead, he simply shakes the creature off into the fire and pays no further attention. Hearing that the governor's father is sick, Paul goes and heals him; whereupon many other sick people are brought to him, and he heals them.

There is no sign, after ten years, that the Gifts and Fruit of the Holy Spirit are diminishing in the lives of those who come to St. Luke's. There has been, of course, a continual renewing as people, week by week, come and receive the Holy Spirit, and begin their new life of freedom and power in the Spirit; but those who have been walking in the Spirit for ten years, if they have continued faithfully to trust Jesus, have attained a greater maturity in their lives, and also have not seen any diminishing of God's miracle-working and prayer-answering power.

On two occasions recently, at St. Luke's, broken wrists have been healed by prayer, and in both cases X-ray tests were taken by doctors before and after, leaving no doubt about the healings. One of these is of particular interest because it happened to Frances, a gracious lady who has been a member of the parish for some forty years. Like a number of "old-timers," she received the Holy Spirit shortly after I came, and has been growing steadily in the Lord ever since. She had the misfortune to fall and injure her wrist. Thinking it was just sprained, she treated it at home for several weeks, but when the pain and swelling did not subside, she went to her doctor, who X-rayed the affected part.

"Why, Frances," he said, with concern, "why didn't you come to me before this? This wrist is broken, and you've let it go so long that I can't set it. You'll have to go to a bone surgeon!" And he made the necessary arrangements. Before the appointment with the specialist, however, Frances came to Christian friends and asked them to pray for her wrist. The bone surgeon looked at the arm and said:

"We'll have to have another X-ray."

When the picture was developed he shook his head wonderingly. "Why, my dear," he said, "there's nothing wrong with

meetings

your wrist!" Jesus had done the work. Frances went straight home and mowed the lawn!

Even more startling was another recent healing. Eleanor came to join the church in 1962. She received Christ as her Saviour, and shortly afterward was baptized in the Holy Spirit. She had had a damaged heart for a long time, and soon after joining our fellowship submitted to open-heart surgery to replace a damaged valve with a plastic one. The results were not satisfactory, and she soon had to have a second open-heart operation, this time to have the plastic unit replaced by a human tissue transplant. In 1968, the heart specialist said to her:

"Eleanor, I'm sorry to have to tell you this, but you're going to have to have another operation on your heart. The valve is becoming defective again."

The night before she was to check in to the hospital for this third surgery, Eleanor was at a meeeting where she heard the testimony of a businessman visiting us from Texas. He had been used by God to bring back to life a man who had been dead for forty-five minutes.* He told of several wonderful healings which had occurred since, due, no doubt, to the tremendous increase of his own faith. At the end of the meeting, this visitor, one of our own laymen, and I prayed for Eleanor with the laying on of hands. The next evening, after she had been in the hospital for her pre-surgical tests, Eleanor telephoned me. She was so excited she could hardly talk, but she managed to say:

"Father Bennett! Praise the Lord! Do you know what happened to me? I checked in to the hospital today, and had all kinds of tests: X-rays, cardiograms, catheterizations, and so forth. Then the doctors on the heart team came in, one by one,

---

* See "In Time for God's Appointment," by Sherwin McCurdy as told to Jamie Buckingham, *Christian Life*, Oct. 1969, p. 40.

and said: 'Eleanor, we don't know what's happened, but there's nothing wrong with you!' Then the chief specialist came in and said: 'Eleanor, I don't understand it, but your heart has returned to normal. You can go to work eight hours a day if you so desire!'" This she proceeded to do, and has been doing so ever since, in vigorous health!

There is obviously *something* different about St. Luke's Church, for not long ago the local morning newspaper, the *Seattle Post-Intelligencer*, devoted most of the front page of their Saturday night final to a report on St. Luke's! Yet St. Luke's is an Episcopal Church in good standing, its church services in keeping with the "doctrine, discipline, and worship of the Protestant Episcopal Church" in the U.S.A. There is a sizable group of licensed lay readers, and the ladies are active in the women's work of the diocese, and some hold or have held important offices. I myself was appointed Dean of our Convocation for two successive years, before finding it necessary to resign due to the pressure of my outside ministry. St. Luke's is regarded by our bishop and other chief ministers as one of the churches that is, as one said to me recently, "going upstream against the current, in a day when many churches are shrinking and dying."

Ten years ago, only a very small group met me at St. Luke's on a Sunday; now five services are held each Sunday, and during the week a large number of people from a variety of denominations come to various other meetings for prayer and instruction, so that our total weekly attendance runs well over two thousand. The vocal gifts of the Spirit, tongues, interpretation, and prophecy, are sometimes manifested at the "family service" on Sunday morning, but there is still a conservative attitude on this, for the people of the parish know that on Sunday morning they are "fishing," rather than "swimming"!

There is plenty of opportunity at other times during the week for more informal sharing in praise and prayer, as for example, on Tuesday night. The several hundred who meet at that time share in enthusiastic gospel singing, praise, prayer, testimony, and teaching, and the tenor of the meeting is relaxed; yet all things are done in "decency and order." Many get together in homes during the week for more times of prayer and praise.

Each Friday evening there is an "information meeting," and in the course of the last ten years, an estimated eight to ten thousand persons have received the Holy Spirit at these meetings. Very few of these have joined St. Luke's, for we have always insisted that they return to their own churches to share what has happened to them. This is why, although the parish has flourished, we have not become a huge congregation. Our membership on the books is still less than a thousand, precisely because we have discouraged people from joining us.

In the last ten years the budget at St. Luke's has increased fourteen times, from $12,000 to $170,000 per annum; yet there are no "drives" for finances. We do not even have an "every-member canvass." No one is approached individually and asked for money, and we do not seek support from those outside the Christian fellowship. We encourage the members of St. Luke's to tithe* their income as a Christian minimum. The people give willingly, because they believe in, and are involved in, the work that their money is supporting. This year the parish will give $24,000 to the support of outside work, missionary and other, through the Diocese of Olympia. There is much additional missionary giving which is hard to assess, because it is given individually, and as the Holy Spirit leads. If a missionary speaks at St. Luke's, and his work commends itself to the listeners, they will support him regardless of his denomination. During the last few years, for example, sub-

* *Tithe* means to give ten per cent of one's income to God's work.

stantial backing has been given to a young Korean Presbyterian, who is doing a wonderful work on the front lines in Vietnam.

In these days, both protestant and Roman Catholic bodies are reporting that thousands of ministers and priests are "bailing out" under the discouragement of the times, and going into other businesses and professions. However, wherever the "charismatic renewal" is in progress, the opposite trend is observed. For the first fifty years of St. Luke's existence, not one man had ever gone into the ministry. In the last ten years, three men have been ordained to the ministry from the membership of St. Luke's; three men are in seminary preparing for the ministry, while three others have been accepted as postulants from the diocese to enter seminary as soon as they have finished their college work. One young woman went into the church army and has since married a minister; another became a deaconess-missionary and is now working in Alaska. Hundreds of people, of course, have gone "into the ministry" right where they live. Most of the personal counselling and praying at St. Luke's is done by lay people; indeed, we regard the parish church as a training centre for lay-ministry.

Physical and organizational growth is not an end in itself. The people of this parish know that a big church does not necessarily mean spiritual success. They are aware that the outward form and organization of the Christian fellowship may change drastically within a short time. For these reasons they have not rushed to build an elaborate new church building.

They know God is not interested in blessing any particular denomination or organization as such. The Church is one: God's people, those who have accepted Jesus and have come alive. On the other hand, God isn't against the "old-line" denominations, but uses them for His purpose if they let themselves be used. The Holy Spirit today is reaching into the structures that man has set up, ignoring our labels, and touching and empowering those who are receptive. What will the Church be like when the Holy Spirit really has His way? None of us know the full answer, but we are catching some exciting glimpses!

The beautiful part about the revival and growth at St. Luke's is that it does not centre around any human person. When the Rector is away—which he often is!—the church flourishes just the same as when he is at home; sometimes better! The work has always been shared, not only with other ministers, but most of all with the people. From the very beginning, one of the great marks of the "charismatic renewal," or Pentecostal revival, in the historic churches, has been that it does not centre on an individual or a group, or any particular denomination. Whenever in the history of the Pentecostal movement any individual or group has tried to gain control, that group or individual has "come a cropper."

Do we have people who do not accept the charismatic renewal, but are still active members of the parish? Yes, we have a number of good folk who, while they are pleased with the new vigour of the church, cannot see the experience of the Baptism of the Holy Spirit for themselves. The experience has in no way been forced upon them, and they see the beneficial effect it as had, both on the corporate life of the church, and on the individual lives of their friends, so they are content to stay.

It is much more difficult to give a brief answer to the question so often asked: "What happens to the social attitudes of the people who have been baptized in the Holy Spirit?" So many earnest people today are convinced that if you believe in an individual experience of salvation through Jesus Christ, you can't possibly be "socially concerned." This, of course, isn't true. When people receive Christ, and the Baptism in the

Holy Spirit, one of the most striking effects in their lives is that they become deeply and truly concerned over their fellow-men, and over the condition of society. However, since at the same time they become much more aware of the reality of God in human affairs, their overall attitude may turn out to be quite different from that of the "social activists" who have perhaps despaired of accomplishing anything through spiritual means, or of believing that God, if He exists at all, really takes any active part in those affairs.

"Social concern" in the Christian is a by-product of the "Fruit" of the Holy Spirit, and it takes a while to grow! The Baptism in the Holy Spirit does not bring an instant answer to social problems. It takes time for the Holy Spirit really to change wrong attitudes, prejudices, etc. Again and again we draw back from the things the Lord desires to accomplish. When the Christian draws back, however, he "loses his blessing" for the time being—he grieves the Spirit. How long will it take the Holy Spirit to bring him to terms? That depends on how deeply entrenched the prejudice or wrong attitude is, how much it touches the false security of the psyche, and other factors. Nonetheless, one could write interminably of healed relationships, saved marriages, changed attitudes in business, deeper concern about others, etc., that have come as a result of the love and power of God working in people's lives. You can't get away with trying to love God and hating your fellow-man at the same time—it just doesn't work!

We know that there is plenty of room for these "fired-up" Christians to get more deeply involved in community action, yet the inclination is already there and the willingness is there. For example, Ballard is an old Scandinavian community, by tradition strongly white and protestant. Feeling the need to break out of this pattern, in 1967 we agreed with Primm Tabernacle Church, an African Methodist Episcopal Church in the south part of the city, to exchange leadership for our Vacation Bible School; so it came about that year that the faculty and one third of the student body of our Vacation Bible School was made up of black Americans, while the opposite was true for the A.M.E. Church. Though this may not sound very daring in this day of get-tough social activism, yet it was interesting and unusual enough for our local Seattle *Times* to print the story on the front page with a four-column picture.

Many unsolved problems at St. Luke's? You bet! But they are ones of action, and not of passivity. The pastoral and other problems at this church are concerned with how to control and guide a fast-moving vehicle, not how to get a lumbering and unwieldy one into motion! The people are eager to serve, but need guidance as to how to do it effectively.

At the very end of Acts 28 we find Paul living in his own hired house, and meeting all who come to him. The Jews—his own countrymen—visit him, and listen with great interest to what he has to say, but when he is finished most of them simply spend their time in learned theological discussion. "The Jews departed, and had great reasoning among themselves." [1]

I was at a meeting in Oregon where one young minister challenged me. He wasn't ungracious; he just didn't agree with my theology. He held a mild debate with me in the presence of others there—mostly businessmen—and then departed, feeling that he had made his point. Shortly after he left, a young businessman asked for and received the Baptism in the Holy Spirit. He was so overcome with the joy of the Lord that he, like others on the Day of Pentecost itself, looked as if he was filled with new wine. I could not miss the sad contrast between the young minister departing in intellectual triumph, but still dry and hungry in his soul, and the young businessman, filled

with the joy which he had accepted from God in simplicity and
trust.

When the power of the Holy Spirit was received at that first
Pentecost, the followers of Jesus were suddenly filled with the
glory of God. Some onlookers thought that they were drunk,
but Peter said:

"They are not drunk, as you suppose, after all, it's only 9
o'clock in the morning! But this is that which the prophet Joel
said would happen: 'And it shall come to pass in the last days,
saith God, that I will pour out of my Spirit upon all flesh . . .' "

The outpouring which began at Pentecost has continued ever
since, and in these days in an ever-increasing flood. We too,
like the young minister, can get so tangled in intellectual ques-
tionings that we may spend all our time having "great reason-
ings among ourselves," and miss the glory of God! The Holy
Spirit is ready to answer our questions if we're ready to listen.
The Book of Acts is open-ended; it's still going on. Your life,
and what you allow God to do in it may yet be another chapter!

Chapter References

Chapter References

CHAPTER I

No references

CHAPTER II

1. *The Book of Common Prayer*, The Ordering of Priests, p. 542
2. Acts 2:4, 8:15–17, 10:46, 19:6
3. *The Book of Common Prayer*, The Order of Confirmation, p. 297
4. *The Book of Common Prayer*, Offices of Instruction, p. 291
5. *Doctrine in the Church of England*, compiled by the Anglican Church, Society for Promoting Christian Knowledge of the Church of England with approval of the Archbishops, 1922–1937, p. 93

CHAPTER III

1. Mark 16:17 (Author's paraphrase)
2. I Corinthians 14:5 (Author's paraphrase)
3. I Corinthians 14:18 (Literal Greek)
4. Romans 8:26 (Author's paraphrase)
5. I Corinthians 14:2 (Author's paraphrase)

CHAPTER IV

1. Philippians 4:4–7 (Authorized Translation)

CHAPTER V

1. Isaiah 6:1–3 (Authorized Translation)
2. Romans 8:15 (Authorized Translation)

CHAPTER VI

1. Matthew 10:8 (Literal Greek)
2. Mark 16:17–18 (Authorized Translation)

CHAPTER VII

No references

CHAPTER VIII

No references

CHAPTER IX

No references

CHAPTER X

1. Acts 2:4 (Authorized Translation)

CHAPTER XI

1. I John 4:20a (Revised Standard)
2. James 2:16a (Revised Standard)

CHAPTER XII

1. Philippians 4:19 (Literal Greek)
2. John 14:12

CHAPTER XIII

1. Romans 8:26 (Author's paraphrase)

CHAPTER XIV

1. Hebrews 6 : 6 (Authorized Translation)

CHAPTER XV

1. Philippians 4 : 19 (Authorized Translation)
2. Ezekiel 24 : 15–18 (Authorized Translation)
3. Isaiah 57 : 1 (Authorized Translation)
4. Romans 8 : 11 (Literal Greek)

CHAPTER XVI

No references

CHAPTER XVII

No references

CHAPTER XVIII

1. *The Book of Common Prayer,* Offices of Instruction, p. 291
2. I Corinthians 12 : 7–11 (Authorized Translation)

CHAPTER XIX

No references

CHAPTER XX

No references

CHAPTER XXI

1. John 14 : 12 (Authorized Translation)

CHAPTER XXII

1. Acts 28 : 29 (Authorized Translation)
2. Acts 2 : 15–17 (Author's paraphrase, first two verses; Authorized Translation, final verse)

Comments and inquiries should be directed to:

The Rev. Dennis J. Bennett

P.O. Box 5212

Seattle, Washington 98107